Air Force Manpower Determinants

Options for More-Responsive Processes

ALBERT A. ROBBERT, LISA M. HARRINGTON, LOUIS T. MARIANO,
SUSAN A. RESETAR, DAVID SCHULKER, JOHN S. CROWN, PAUL EMSLIE,
SEAN MANN, GARY MASSEY

Prepared for the United States Air Force
Approved for public release; distribution unlimited

 PROJECT AIR FORCE

For more information on this publication, visit www.rand.org/t/RR4420

Library of Congress Cataloging-in-Publication Data is available for this publication.

ISBN: 978-1-9774-0484-8

Support RAND

Make a tax-deductible charitable contribution at
www.rand.org/giving/contribute

www.rand.org

Preface

The Air Force has long-standing processes and resources in place to develop determinants of the manpower required for Air Force activities. These processes often entail extensive measurement of work and workload in order to determine the appropriate relationships between workforce size and expected workloads. The validity of the derived relationships at the time they are developed is generally considered acceptable. However, the level of effort required to develop them is extensive. Given resource limitations, the processes currently in use are unable to keep up with the demand for new determinants and update of existing determinants necessitated by changes in mission and technology. Moreover, longstanding methods and conventions warrant periodic review to identify potentially more-accurate assessments of manpower needs. The purpose of this project is to identify and evaluate options to increase the responsiveness of these processes or, if sufficient options are not available, to depict the increased resources needed to meet the demand.

The research reported here was commissioned by the Deputy Under Secretary of the Air Force, Management and the Deputy Chief of Staff for Manpower, Personnel, and Services, U.S. Air Force and conducted within the Manpower, Personnel, and Training Program of RAND Project AIR FORCE as part of a fiscal year 2018 project, Air Force Manpower Availability and Determinant Factors.

This report should be of value to members of the Air Force human resource management community concerned with determination of manpower requirements and to commanders, functional managers, and others whose missions depend critically on appropriate sizing of their workforces.

RAND Project AIR FORCE

RAND Project AIR FORCE (PAF), a division of the RAND Corporation, is the U.S. Air Force's federally funded research and development center for studies and analyses. PAF provides the Air Force with independent analyses of policy alternatives affecting the development, employment, combat readiness, and support of current and future air, space, and cyber forces. Research is conducted in four programs: Strategy and Doctrine; Force Modernization and Employment; Manpower, Personnel, and Training; and Resource Management. The research reported here was prepared under contract FA7014-16-D-1000.

Additional information about PAF is available on our website:
http://www.rand.org/paf/

This report documents work originally shared with the U.S. Air Force on September 27, 2018. The draft report, issued in September 2018, was reviewed by formal peer reviewers and U.S. Air Force subject-matter experts.

Contents

Figures

Tables

Summary

An important function of Air Force personnel management organizations is to determine manpower requirements. The Air Force has long-standing processes and resources for determining the manpower required for Air Force activities. These detailed and complex processes measure workloads and use the data to determine the workforce needed to accomplish the work. The Air Force asked RAND Project AIR FORCE to examine these processes and to identify and evaluate options to increase their efficiency. We found that the processes themselves are comprehensive and technically sophisticated but are less efficient and effective than they could be. Thus, our review suggested a number of steps that the Air Force could take toward improvement.

The Air Force uses many processes, including crew ratios and the Logistics Composite Model, to determine manpower requirements. In the research underlying this document, we focused primarily on one type of determinant, *manpower standards*, primarily as used for agile combat support (ACS) requirements in the active component. The manpower standard is used to determine either the number of personnel required for a type of work center or function—for example, for a Security Forces squadron or a force support squadron. Other factors, such as indirect work and overtime, are also incorporated in calculations used to develop a standard. The standard, which is expressed in required monthly man-hours, is then applied to individual work centers to determine the manpower required in each.

Prior RAND Corporation research found that some manpower standards are old enough to raise questions about their continued viability. Manning resource shortfalls within Air Force requirements squadrons have been identified as a major limiting factor in the ability to update manpower standards on a timely basis. This concern was echoed at a September 2017 Workforce Summit convened by the Vice Chief of Staff of the Air Force, which provided motivation for this research.

In this research, we sought to find new approaches to address these issues and to identify changes in the resources needed to implement them. The underlying research provided case studies of manpower modeling practices in other organizations. It examined the development of Air Force manpower standards and the factors used in converting workload estimates to manpower requirements. It also examined several limitations of current processes—the limited influence of manpower standards on programming decisions, the lack of manpower credit for deployment demands, the limited availability of feedback on manpower adequacy, and the limited analytic competencies of the workforce dedicated to developing manpower standards.

To pursue our investigation, we interviewed relevant Air Force staffs and representatives of other military, government, and private-sector organizations to gain an understanding of their workforce sizing practices. We also reviewed the relevant academic literature and available Air

Force sources, including manpower standards, Air Force instructions, and data from the Manpower Programming and Execution System. We also observed workshops and other activities the Air Force uses in its process and, when appropriate, conducted data analysis and simulations.

What Other Organizations Do Well

Our review of the approaches other military services, government agencies, and private industry use suggested that common methodologies for determining workforce demand are comparable to those the Air Force already uses. However, industry's competitive pressures and profit motive result in significant differences in how workforce demand is determined for the enterprise as a whole—with workforce size determined as part of a larger business case analysis. Thus, private-sector organizations assess their workforce requirements more frequently and, because they have more flexibility to manage workforces than the military does, also make frequent adjustments. For these reasons and also because of the very different requirements for transparency in government organizations, we determined that the private sector offers limited insight for the Air Force into transferable enterprisewide approaches for determining manpower requirements.

The best examples we found of effective processes were those for generating requirements for Army force (support) functions and Navy shore installation functions. In both cases, task time and frequency data are collected as a basis for workforce requirements models. However, in both cases, data are collected primarily through virtual processes (video conferences, data-collection tools) rather than in face-to-face workshops with subject-matter experts (SMEs). These virtual processes improve accuracy because they enable larger sample sizes, provide clear instructions on how to estimate task times and frequency, and provide an opportunity to follow up on outliers or clearly identify the need for variances. Air Force manpower policy and guidance permit a similar methodology; however, during our research period, Air Force manpower requirements squadrons (MRSs) primarily employed workshops for measurement.

Further, we found that both the Army and the Navy expect force-generating and installation-support organizations to develop and articulate their own manpower requirements. The Navy has two commands with installation-support responsibilities, each with its own manpower function. The Army has many functional commands (with responsibilities somewhat akin to those of Air Force functional managers) with force generating responsibilities and their own respective command manpower experts. However, the Army also has an agency (the U.S. Army Manpower Analysis Agency) that serves a consulting and certification function. The Air Force, by policy, holds functions responsible for manpower standards but, in practice, holds the Air Force Manpower Analysis Agency (AFMAA) and the Directorate of Manpower, Organization, and Resources responsible for initiating and managing most assessments and producing defensible standards. In the view of Air Force manpower managers, some Air Force functions tend to view updates of their manpower standards as potential threats to existing resources and are, thus, reluctant to embrace the process, particularly if it yields evidence of overresourcing. The current relationship allows functional managers to exercise a veto of any change or update of a manpower standard by withholding their coordination on or approval of the standard.

Manpower Standard Development

Our investigation into the standard-development process uncovered opportunities for improvement. Multiple sources of measurement error and modeling deficiencies may cause imprecise estimates of manpower requirements. Specifically, estimation of task times is error prone, and methods are insufficient to minimize prediction error. We found that much of an MRS staff's effort is expended on administrative and nonmanpower tasks. Given practices in other services and available technology, we also found that the face-to-face workshops with SMEs are not the appropriate primary vehicle for significant process improvement.

To improve manpower standard development, we

- highly endorse exploring an ongoing survey approach similar to the one the Navy uses for collecting task times and frequencies
- recommend that AFMAA benchmark this approach with the Navy, adapt it for Air Force use, then test it with actual manpower studies to evaluate and expand as warranted.

We saw room for improvement in manpower-standard modeling and recommend the following:

- Whenever feasible, derive regression estimates from all applicable locations, not just those represented by SMEs at workshops.
- For functions in which a poor linear relationship between workloads and workload factors is found, consider nonlinear models and machine learning or artificial intelligence approaches.
- Use regression or other methods in lieu of the ratio method.
- Observe statistical best practices for any model used in developing a manpower standard.
- Hold functional managers responsible for their standards, and require AFMAA certification of manpower standards.

Holding functional managers effectively responsible for their standards, somewhat as we observed in the Army and Navy functional commands, could realize several advantages. Process mapping, development of standard work documents, and continuous process improvement could be clearly defined as functional managers' responsibilities and could become prerequisites for constructing or updating a standard. Functional managers could choose among several sources for developing their standards—AFMAA analysts, contract consultants, or their own staffs. The motivation for functional managers to maintain a valid, up-to-date standard could be established through a policy that programming processes could use a standard to justify resources only if it is certified by AFMAA and that lack of an AFMAA-certified standard would jeopardize resources in the programming process. Standards could be reviewed periodically (e.g., every two to three years) and would be subject to decertification if mission or technological changes significantly altered their included workload factors.

Management Engineering Workforce

Other organizations in both the public and private sectors tend to accomplish data collection and modeling using workforces that are typically qualified at a professional level. Their educational qualifications run more toward management engineering and operations research, and their experience levels tend to be high. While the Air Force AFMAA and MRS civilian workforces tend to have similarly high levels of experience, we found analytic skills to be thinly available, particularly among the noncommissioned officers (NCOs) and former NCOs reemployed as civilians, and we found that the NCO components have very low levels of experience because of their relatively brief tenures in MRSs. The Air Force's reliance on what is largely a paraprofessional management engineering workforce may be due to its greater emphasis on workshop scheduling and conduct, data gathering, coordination of results, and similar tasks rather than on data analysis and model formulation.

Several arguments surfaced to support the need for an NCO contingent in the management engineering workforce. One argument is the need for deployable resources. However, we found deployment demands for manpower specialists at AFMAA and the MRSs during our study period to be low. Another is the need for familiarity with the functions being studied. However, we found that the chances of an NCO being asked to study a function in which he or she had previous experience was very slim. Additionally, if a civilianized AFMAA continued to employ large numbers of veterans, diverse functional experiences would still be available in the workforce.

We also question the rationale for dispersal of the workforce among AFMAA and three MRSs. The Air Force should review the distribution of the manpower workforce to optimize mission accomplishment and interaction with functional communities. Consolidation at a single location could yield economies of scale and may increase analytic rigor and consistency. Properly addressing where physical presence today is most beneficial and considering a move toward virtual rather than face-to-face measurement processes may provide AFMAA more-logical options to locate personnel than the present dispersal.

To improve capability of the management engineering workforce, we recommend

- professionalizing the management engineering workforce by shifting more NCO positions to civilians and classifying a much larger proportion of positions in analytic job series, with their attendant education requirements
- to provide greater retention and development of needed experience within the civilian workforce, establishing career paths such that positions are career-ladder graded, with entry at grade GS-7 and automatic promotions to GS-9 and GS-11 at specified intervals, contingent on acceptable performance.

Availability Factors and Other Adjustments

Most sources of nonavailable time, such as for leave or temporary duty, are captured objectively and with timely updates in man-hour availability factors. However, we found some sources are not adequately accounted for, which can result in over- or underestimations of manpower availability. The most commonly voiced concern was about deployments from garrison forces, but, in our judgment, man-hour availability factors are not the appropriate place to capture nonavailability due to deployment—so we propose an alternative in the next section. We also found that nonavailability due to "family days" and permissive temporary duty (e.g., for house hunting or family leave) are not currently captured but that efforts are being made to identify suitable data sources for them.

The Air Force has applied the overload factor, used originally in conjunction with rounding rules to prevent undue per-position burdens associated with overtime in small units, in a way that effectively creates a 43-hour workweek as the basis for military manpower requirements. This leaves either less available overtime capacity or a higher level of workforce stress resulting from fluctuations in workload, workforce availability, or shortages due to resource constraints. To resolve this problem,

- we recommend greater transparency in the method of accounting for overtime. The Air Force needs to either recognize the 43-hour workweek or fully account for additional authorizations for a 40-hour week, recognizing the risks of each alternative and considering policy and programming changes to mitigate the risks. Immediate revision of the overload factor to its previous form would increase the number of unfunded authorizations as manpower standards are reapplied. The unfunded authorizations would then compete for resources.

Deployment Credit

Since 2014, deployments have effectively reduced garrison manpower by about 5,000 spaces, with even larger impacts in earlier years. Air Force manpower policies have provisions for deployment credit, but they were not implemented because of the resources required to fund the additional manpower and because they provided only static resources to offset dynamically shifting requirements. As a result, decades of continuous deployment demand have resulted in varying levels of workforce stress, degraded garrison service levels, or some combination of the two. Our findings suggest that, in ACS functions at the wing level, year-to-year deployment demand can be forecast, and deployments can thus be accommodated using an approach we termed *dynamic deployment credit*. In addition, the turnover that normal assignment and separation processes create can, to a reasonable approximation in most circumstances, keep personnel resources aligned with the manpower changes associated with dynamic credits. To provide deployment credit, we recommend that the Air Force

- establish a pool of dynamically shifted authorizations to be placed in units during periods of projected deployment taskings. The pool could be managed by the same officials responsible for assigning deployment taskings (currently the Air Force Personnel Center), with normal rotational assignments and separations used to keep strengths in line with fluctuating unit-level requirements. We found enough stability and predictability in deployment taskings to make this approach feasible, particularly for high-density requirements.

Feedback Loops and Resourcing

In a systems-theory context, Air Force manpower determinants are used to estimate the manpower inputs needed to produce airpower and other related Air Force mission-related outputs. With the resources available for manpower measurement being scarce, the Air Force must choose where to apply its capacity for updating manpower standards. Ideally, these choices would be guided by feedback loops.

Our experience with Air Force manpower processes suggest that there is a lack of objective, systematic feedback loops for determining whether adequate manpower requirements are being established. Available feedback comes largely through the impressions formed and unsystematically conveyed by commanders and functional managers. To create more objective, systematic feedback loops, we recommend the Air Force

- use time on the job and performance metrics, in tandem, for feedback. Use a survey approach to capture time on the job for military members; ongoing occupational measurement surveys would serve as a good vehicle for collecting the data. Another useful feedback loop would be the performance metrics associated with Common Output Level Standards, although some of these require improvement to be useful for this purpose.

We found that, under current practices, a manpower standard has minimal effect on the programming of manpower resources.[1] A manpower standard is applied when it is first developed but doing so generally changes only unfunded authorizations. Manpower managers at major commands rarely reapply standards, perceiving, accurately, that changes generally will occur only in unfunded requirements and that unfunded requirements are not routinely used to assess risk and influence programming or policy decisions (as we believe they should be). We recommend the Air Force

- make unfunded authorizations routinely visible in programming processes, levying clear expectations, as appropriate, on manpower managers, functional managers, or programmers at the Air Staff and major commands to take such actions as changing work

---

[1] Requirements derived from manpower standards do not immediately or directly translate into demand for personnel resources. The programming and budgeting processes intervene. These processes are conducted through the Air Force's multilevel corporate structure (Air Force Guidance Memorandum 2018-90-01, 2018).

requirements in the standard work document, explicitly reducing levels of service, adopting a longer workweek, increasing funded authorizations, or directing other resources (civilian employees, contractors, or reservist man-days) to the function.

- To enable more-frequent reapplication of standards, streamline the process by embedding models in updatable tools and displaying unfunded requirements at the aggregate or abbreviated requirement level of detail.

Summary

We recognize that addressing the inefficiencies uncovered in the management engineering processes for ACS functions will take time, effort, and resources. However, rather than abandoning these processes, we believe the Air Force's interests would be best served by taking available steps to make the process more effective, efficient, and relevant to programming decisions.

Acknowledgments

We would like to thank several people in the Air Force for their consideration and guidance in developing and conducting this research. Our work could not have succeeded without their support and cooperation. First and foremost, we thank our primary sponsor, Michelle LoweSolis (Assistant Deputy under Secretary of the Air Force, Management, and Assistant Deputy Chief Management Officer) for hosting a series of "deep dives" into the intricacies of Air Force manpower management. We would also like to thank Vince Gassaway (Deputy Director, Manpower, Organization, and Resources, Deputy Chief of Staff for Manpower and Personnel), Jeffrey Mayo (Deputy Assistant Secretary of the Air Force for Force Management Integration), and Greg Parsons (Director of Plans and Integration, Deputy Chief of Staff for Manpower and Personnel) and their staffs for accompanying us through those deep dives and sharing their insights. Barry Wooding (Office of the Chief Management Officer), Gregory Parton (Directorate of Manpower, Organization, and Resources), and Dennis Carter (Air Force Manpower Analysis Agency [AFMAA]) provided continuous support and technical assistance.

Additionally, we would like to thank the AFMAA personnel who assisted with this research effort, including David Moen for assisting with our study of manpower factors and John Simpson (Chief, Study Management and Quality Assurance Branch) for facilitating and coordinating access to manpower requirements squadrons' staffs and workshops.

We would like to thank the manpower requirements squadrons' commanders, flight chiefs, technical directors, and study leads for their willingness to share their time, knowledge, and insights with us on the manpower determination process and for allowing us to observe workshops, enriching our understanding of how this process works in practice. These discussions and experiences were critically important to our research.

We would like to thank the workforce planners at the Federal Bureau of Investigation, Transportation Security Agency, and Fairfax County Government and in the private sector for engaging with us on their workforce planning activities and approaches. These individuals gave generously of their time and provided contexts and material that were invaluable for understanding how other organizations determine workforce size.

The sister services' manpower planners at the U.S. Army Manpower Analysis Agency, U. S. Fleet Forces Command, and Navy Installations Command patiently explained their services' contexts, organizational structure, methods, and tools. These discussions identified valuable lessons and opportunities for improving Air Force processes.

We appreciate the invaluable context and perspectives that can only be acquired from decades of experience that were provided through discussions with Brian Norman, manpower consultant and former AFMAA Commander; Robert Corsi, RAND adjunct and former Assistant

Deputy Chief of Staff, Manpower, Personnel and Services; and William Booth, Director, Defense Human Resources Activity.

We would also like to thank our colleagues at RAND, including Raymond Conley for his valuable insights and support and Barbara Bicksler for her help in organizing and communicating our results. Finally, many thanks go to our reviewers, James Hosek and Brian Norman, who helped us refine our focus and better shape our message, resulting in a clearer, stronger report. The contributions of these individuals greatly improved the quality of the document.

Abbreviations

ACC	Air Combat Command
ACS	agile combat support
AEF	air and space expeditionary force
AETC	Air Education and Training Command
AF/A1M	Directorate of Manpower, Organization, and Resources
AFI	Air Force Instruction
AFIMSC	Air Force Installation and Mission Support Center
AFMAA	Air Force Manpower Analysis Agency
AFMAN	Air Force Manual
AFPC	Air Force Personnel Center
AFR	Air Force Reserve
AFSC	Air Force specialty code
AGR	active Guard and Reserve
AMC	Air Mobility Command
ANG	Air National Guard
AR	Army Regulation
ART	air reserve technician
ASA(MR&A)	Assistant Secretary of the Army Office of Manpower Requirements and Analysis
CMAT	Command Manpower Analysis Team
CNIC	Commander, Navy Installations Command
CNO	Chief of Naval Operations
COLS	Common Output Level Standards
CONUS	continental United States
CPI	continuous process improvement
CV	coefficient of variation
DIRMS	Data Input Requirements for a Manpower Study

DoD	U.S. Department of Defense
FBI	Federal Bureau of Investigation
FSL	funded staff level
FTE	full-time equivalent
FY	fiscal year
GS	General Schedule (civilian federal government pay scales)
IAF	indirect allowance factor
IMA	individual mobilization augmentee
LCOM	Logistics Composite Model
MAJCOM	major command (Air Force)
MAF	man-hour availability factor
MFT	mission, function, and task
MPES	Manpower Programming and Execution System
MRS	manpower requirements squadron
MSI	manpower standard implementation [code]
NCO	noncommissioned officer
OLF	overload factor
OPNAVINST	Office of the Chief of Naval Operations Instruction
PCS	permanent change of station
PF&D	personal needs, fatigue, and unavoidable delays
PTDY	permissive temporary duty
PWS	performance work statement
R^2	coefficient of determination
RPO	Resource Planning Office (FBI)
SCE	Southern California Edison
SME	subject-matter expert
SMR	statement of manpower requirements
TDA	table of distribution and allowances
TR	traditional reservist

TSA	Transportation Security Agency
USAMAA	U.S. Army Manpower Analysis Agency
USFF	U.S. Fleet Forces Command
UTC	unit type code
WISN	Workload Indicators of Staffing Need

1. Introduction

Background

Air Force manpower requirements—specifications of the human resources required to conduct Air Force missions—are determined through processes that vary somewhat across functional areas and the active and reserve components.[1] For many functions, a first step is development of a *model* or *standard* to determine either the number of personnel or the man-hours of effort required for a type of work center, usually as a function of one or more workload drivers. The model or standard is then applied to individual work centers to determine the manpower each requires. Factors are then applied to account for indirect work (work that must be done but does not directly relate to the work center producing an end product) and for accepted levels of overtime work. When the result is expressed in man-hours per month, a *man-hour availability factor (MAF)*, indicating the average monthly hours a worker is available for primary duties, must be used to determine the number of personnel required. A *manpower determinant* typically includes a manpower table that prescribes the recommended grades and skills needed, given the calculated number of workers required. The results are considered manpower requirements, which can be then depicted on Air Force unit manpower documents as *unfunded* or *funded* manpower requirements; a *funded* manpower requirement is otherwise known as a *manpower authorization*.[2]

Previous RAND Corporation research (Robbert et al., 2014) found that some manpower standards are old enough to raise questions regarding their continued validity. That research found that underresourcing of manpower requirements squadrons (MRSs) was a major factor limiting the updating of manpower standards. Additionally, although deployment demands

---

[1] Air Force Instruction (AFI) 38-201, 2014, p. 92, defines *manpower requirements* as the

> human resources needed to accomplish a specified job, workload, mission, or program. There are two types of manpower requirements: funded and unfunded. Funded manpower requirements are those that have been validated and allocated. Unfunded requirements are validated manpower needs that have been deferred because of budgetary constraints. Manpower requirements are generally determined by an Air Force Manpower Standard or other management decision.

[2] Requirements derived from manpower standards do not immediately or directly translate into demand for personnel resources. The programming and budgeting processes intervene. These processes are conducted through the Air Force's multilevel corporate structure (Air Force Guidance Memorandum 2018-90-01, 2018). AFI 38-101, 2019, p. 170, defines *manpower authorization* as a "funded manpower requirement with detail that defines the position in terms of its function, organization, location, skill, grade, and other appropriate characteristics which commands use to extend end strength resources to units."

appear to be significant in many functions, previous provisions to account for recurring deployment demands in developing manpower standards appear to have been seldom used.[3]

At a September 2017 Workforce Summit, convened by the Vice Chief of Staff of the Air Force, participants representing major commands and functional areas agreed that current processes for updating manpower requirements do not keep pace with changing demands. Additionally, participants indicated that, in planning, programming, and budgeting deliberations, the manpower system provides too little feedback regarding the risks to missions. They saw the need for more-agile manpower processes and were willing to accept less precision in return for greater timeliness.

In the research reported in this document, we sought to find new approaches to address these issues and to identify changes in resources needed to implement them. The underlying research provided case studies of manpower modeling practices in other organizations. It examined the development of Air Force manpower standards and the factors used in converting workload estimates to manpower requirements. We also examined several limitations of current processes: the limited influence of manpower standards on programming decisions, the lack of manpower credit for deployment demands, the limited availability of feedback on manpower adequacy, and the limited analytic competencies of the workforce dedicated to developing manpower standards.

Our initial discussions with Air Force manpower officials led us to conclude that the primary focus of concern was *agile combat support* (ACS)—defined in this context as "the foundational and crosscutting capability to field, base, protect, support, and sustain Air Force forces across the range of military operations" (Air Force Doctrine, Annex 4-0, 2015, p. 2). For ACS, the primary means of relating required manpower to required workloads is the development of *Air Force manpower standards*. A manpower standard expresses required monthly man-hours in a local functional activity as a function of one or more workload drivers. The application of a manpower standard requires using a *MAF* and an *overload factor* to convert monthly man-hours to full-time equivalent (FTE) manpower.[4] Collectively, these constructs were the primary focus of this project.

Methodologies

We first sought to understand current Air Force manpower processes through meetings with current staff of the Air Force Directorate of Manpower, Organization, and Resources (AF/A1M), the Air Force Manpower Analysis Agency (AFMAA), several former MRS commanders, and

---

[3] A superseded Air Force publication devoted to standard manpower practices and procedures provided computation methods for deployment credit (Air Force Manual [AFMAN] 38-208 Vol. I, 2002, pp. 107–110). Its successor publication, AFMAN 38-10, 2019, does not mention deployment credit.

[4] Definitions for the italicized manpower terms in this paragraph can be found in AFI 38-101, 2019, pp. 168–171. The MAF is defined as "the average number of man-hours per month an assigned individual is available to do assigned duties." The overload factor "realizes Air Force leadership's expectation that some overtime is an effective tool instead of adding additional manpower requirements."

others. Additionally, we reviewed a sample of manpower standards, the reports that documented their development, the procedural manuals that guide their development (AFMAN 38-208 Vol. I, 2007; AFMAN 38-208 Vol. II, 2003; AFMAN 38-102, 2019 [which superseded the three volumes of AFMAN 38-208]; AFI 38-101, 2019 [which superseded AFI 38-201]), and suggestions for streamlining the manpower determination processes AFMAA solicits from the Air Force manpower community. We also observed workshops and other activities used by the Air Force in its processes.

We reviewed pertinent literature and conducted a series of interviews to gain an understanding of common industrial engineering techniques and other military, government, and private-sector organizations' practices regarding workforce sizing. We also examined relevant literature regarding the accuracy and dynamics of time estimation by humans. We built a simulation model of the processes for estimating required manpower to more fully inform sources of estimation error. In addition to reviewing manpower determinant processes, we also evaluated MAFs using data derived from Air Force personnel data files. While the latter entailed some quantitative analysis, the analysis leading to most of our findings was largely qualitative.

Organization of the Report

Chapter 2 briefly describes current processes for developing manpower standards, including mathematical specifications of the key elements of a standard. Chapter 3 describes comparable practices in private-sector, public-sector, and other military organizations. Chapter 4 delves more deeply into the processes used to develop the man-hour estimates used in manpower standards. Chapter 5 examines man-hour availability and other factors used to convert man-hour estimates to FTE manpower requirements. Chapter 6 examines a potential process for providing manpower credit for deployment demands. Chapter 7 explores possibilities for incorporating feedback loops that would provide indicators of the adequacy of applied manpower standards. Chapter 8 provides observations on the composition of the workforce that the Air Force uses to develop manpower standards. Chapter 9 presents our conclusions and recommendations. Three appendixes provide supplementary information.

2. Current Methods for Determining Manpower Requirements

Robbert et al., 2014, described the standard tools and processes the Air Force uses to determine manpower requirements. These include manpower standards, crew ratios, the Logistics Composite Model (LCOM), technical estimates, deployment requirements expressed in unit type codes (UTCs), headquarters staff strength ceilings, procedures for individual mobilization augmentee (IMA) requirements, in-house versus contractor competitions in keeping with Office of Management and Budget Circular A-76, and other minor processes. Any such process used to calculate manpower requirements is referred to as a *manpower determinant*. In the research underlying this document, we focused primarily on one type of determinant, manpower standards, primarily as used for ACS requirements in the active component.[1] This prioritization was driven by a major stimulus for the research: the findings of the September 2017 Workforce Summit discussed in Chapter 1.

Requirements Process Coverage

Within the Manpower Programming and Execution System (MPES), a *manpower standard implementation* (MSI) code is associated with each authorization to indicate the type of determinant or other approach used to develop the manpower requirement.[2] Table 2.1, which updates the comparable table provided in Robbert et al., 2014, contains the requirements process coverage by workforce category. Appendix A contains a list of MSI codes, their mapping to the processes listed in Table 2.1, and a count of authorizations carrying each MSI code. These data indicate that, for the active component, manpower standards account for a large proportion of requirements covered by standard processes. While crew ratios and LCOM also cover large numbers of active component requirements, our research sponsors agreed that maintenance of those determinants is less problematic than maintenance of manpower standards and technical estimates. We thus excluded these from our focus. For full-time requirements in the reserve components—civilians, active Guard and Reserve (AGR), air reserve technicians (ARTs) in the Air Force Reserve (AFR), technicians in the Air National Guard (ANG)—manpower standards

---

[1] A *manpower standard* is defined as the "basic tool used to determine the most effective and efficient level of manpower required to support a function. It is a quantitative expression that represents a work center's man-hour requirements in response to varying levels of workload" (AFI 38-101, 2019, p. 170).

[2] MPES is a database containing detailed information on each actual (funded) or potential (unfunded) manpower position within the Air Force. Primary responsibility for updating the detailed information rests with the major commands to which manpower has been allocated.

Table 2.1. Requirements Process Coverage by Workforce Categories

Workforce Category	Manpower Standard	Crew Ratio	LCOM	Technical Estimate	UTC	Headquarters Staffs	IMA	Other	No Standard Process	Total
Active military	93,248	11,330	42,491	30,285		31,383		1,060	84,395	294,192
Active civilian	36,517	10	1,425	11,260		17,372		4,787	76,740	148,111
AFR civilian	2,336		78	8	1	716			645	3,784
ANG civilian	255					0		0	447	702
AFR AGR	1,229	172			449	614	4		766	3,234
ANG AGR	11,343	1			143	704		17	2,751	14,959
AFR ART	3,548	63	2,216	77	13	182			4,196	10,295
ANG technician	18,839		590			433		129	2,628	22,619
AFR TR	34	3,798	7,105	178	35,697	423			8,292	55,527
ANG TR	279				86,174	1,536	1	124	3,298	91,412
AFR IMA						1	8,225		0	8,226
Total	167,628	15,374	53,905	41,808	122,477	53,364	8,230	6,117	184,158	653,061

SOURCE: MPES data extract from September 2017.
NOTES: Includes funded authorizations only and excludes permanent party student authorizations. Some MSI coding errors are apparent in the data, such as citing manpower standards as a basis for TR positions or the IMA MSI for active military or AGR positions.

are also the predominant form of coverage. For part-time traditional reservists (TRs), requirements are, by policy, predominantly based on UTCs.[1]

Developing Manpower Standards

Air Force manpower standards are developed using an approach described in AFMAN 38-102, 2019. The scope of a standard or other manpower determinant is a *function*, defined as

> A group of personnel that use similar machines, processes, methods, and operations to do homogeneous work usually located in a centralized area. (AFM 38-102, 2019, p. 336)

Examples include the military personnel section of a force support squadron, a Security Forces squadron, or a base-level financial management organization. The full approach includes process improvement steps prior to development of a manpower standard for the optimized process design. Our focus is primarily on the standard itself.

While the techniques used in developing a standard can vary depending on the nature of the function, the following steps were described in AFMAN 38-208 Vol. I, 2007, pp. 50–78 (since superseded):

- **Develop a process-oriented description.** A *process* is a series of value-added actions that bring about an end or result. Processes are the basic building blocks that are measured in building the standard.
- **Identify potential workload factors.** These are exogenous, programmable drivers of workload for the function being studied. Examples include base population, number of authorized aircraft, space-based systems supported, vehicles supported, flying hours, or students.
- **Measure the required work.** This typically includes determining the average time required for a qualified worker to perform a complete cycle of each process and the average cycle frequency for each process. It may be accomplished through field measurements, workshops involving subject-matter experts (SMEs), or both.
- **Analyze the data.** This step includes refining the available work and workload measurements to be used in formulating the standard.
- **Develop a model.** A common modeling approach is to regress the measured work (in monthly man-hours, summed across all processes) at each measured location on the counts of workload factors at each location during the measured period.
- **Account for variances.** These are positive or negative adjustments to core manpower requirements to account for work that is not accomplished at all locations.

A manpower standard for a work center is typically expressed as a linear equation in the form

$$y_i = a + x_i b,$$

---

[1] UTCs specify personnel and equipment to be included in deployment packages assembled for specific functional capabilities. Combatant commanders use UTCs to express their deployment requirements in wartime planning and execution. As discussed in Robbert et al., 2014, this policy is not in force.

where

y_i = required man-hours per month in the work center at location i

a = an intercept term, typically estimated using multiple regression

b = a vector of coefficients, also estimated using multiple regression

x_i = a vector of current or projected workload factors in the work center at location i.

The sum-product of b and x_i is the variable cost of manpower at each location, while a is the fixed cost common to all locations. Location-specific variances may add to or subtract from this calculation.

Determining Requirements

The manpower standard for a work center must be applied at each of the work center's locations, using workload factors specific to the location, to determine local requirements. As discussed in the following subsections, several adjustments are required to determine the requirement.

Indirect Allowance Factor

A manpower standard typically yields the number of man-hours per month required for direct work, which consists of tasks that pertain directly to functional end products. Indirect work—tasks common to all work centers, not readily identifiable with a work center's specific product or service—must also be accounted for. While Air Force manpower processes allow measurement of indirect work in unique circumstances, a factor of 6.19 percent of direct man-hours is considered applicable in most circumstances (AFMAN 38-102, 2019, p. 272).

Personal, Fatigue, and Delay Allowance Factor

For standards based on strictly measured cycle times, an allowance factor for personal needs, fatigue, and unavoidable delays (PF&D) is used to account for unavoidable absences from productive effort. Unless otherwise justified, factor of 1.067 (i.e., 6.7 percent) is used, based on two 15-minute breaks in an 8-hour day (AFMAN 38-102, 2019, p. 118).

$$\frac{480 \text{ minutes}}{480 \text{ minutes} - 39 \text{ minutes}} = 1.067.$$

Man-Hour Availability Factors

A final step in applying a manpower standard is to convert required man-hours per month in a work center to FTE positions required. This is done by dividing the required man-hours by one or more MAFs. The MAF accounts for the portion of monthly duty time that is unavailable for normal duties because of such factors as holidays, vacation, sickness, training, and relocation. The military 40-hour workweek MAF is 148.79 hours per month (AFMAA, 2017); the comparable civilian MAF is 143.48 hours for employees based in the continental United States (CONUS) and 148.59 hours for those based overseas (Air Force Personnel Center [AFPC], 2013b). Alternative MAFs are calculated for extended workweeks, such as those that firefighters (72-hour workweek) or personnel stationed in Korea (48-hour workweek) experience (AFPC, 2013a). For work centers with both military and civilian workforces, the convention is to use the military MAF for military-essential work, then use the civilian MAF for remaining work.

Overload Factor

An overload factor is normally used to reduce total manpower requirements, recognizing that the Air Force expects some overtime to offset manpower requirements (AFI 38-101, 2019, p. 23). For a military work center under a 40-hour workweek, a factor of 7.7 percent is used (i.e., the MAF is multiplied by 1.077), which translates into assuming that the average worker will contribute 11.5 hours of overtime per month.

Calculating a Requirement

When applying a manpower standard to determine the number of authorizations in a specific work center at a specific location, the calculation will generally take the following form:

$$y^p = \frac{y^h \times \text{IAF} \times \text{PF\&D}}{\text{OLF} \times \text{MAF}},$$

where

y^p = required positions in a work center

y^h = direct man-hours per month required in the work center

IAF = indirect allowance factor

OLF = overload factor.

The result of this calculation is rounded up. However, see discussion of the overload factor and its relationship to rounding in Chapter 5.

Variances

In some cases, manpower requirements are driven by factors that are not common to all locations. In these cases, one or more *variances*, in the form of equations linked to the unique workload factors or similar determinants, are provided as supplements to the basic manpower standard. For example, students at training centers present base support requirements that differ significantly from those presented by permanent party (i.e., nonstudent) personnel at the training center location. For manpower standards that use base population as a workload factor, the basic manpower standard uses the count of permanent party personnel as the workload factor, while a variance uses average student population as a factor.

3. Practices in Other Organizations

The military is not unique in its need to understand and develop workforce requirements. Organizations in both the public and private sectors use various approaches to determine enterprisewide workforce requirements, some of which are described in this chapter. In investigating how other organizations approach this challenge, we looked especially for practices that the Air Force might be able to adapt to improve its practices for developing manpower standards or other determinants. We gathered information in two ways: through a review of the academic and professional literatures on determining workforce requirements and through interviews with persons responsible for manpower management or staffing in select government and private-sector organizations.

Approaches for Determining Workforce Requirements Discussed in the Literature

We found little evidence in the literature that private-sector organizations develop empirically derived relationships between workforce requirements and workload factors comparable to Air Force manpower standards.[1] The large majority of organizations develop workforce demand forecasts as a part of the overall workforce planning process (depicted in Figure 3.1). Typically guided by a headquarters or corporate-level management team and driven by individual business units or agencies, workforce planning involves identifying how strategic goals and objectives (or new missions) affect forecasts of workforce demand and supply (in terms of the numbers of individuals and required knowledge and skills) to ensure the workforce can support the goals and objectives identified in the strategy.

Workforce supply forecasts take into account the numbers and skills of employees, and projections of attrition; workforce demand forecasts consider internal and external factors that affect the characteristics of the needed workforce. These factors can include general economic conditions, plans for new product lines, needed workforce skills, and the composition and skills of available workforces among others. Gaps between forecast workforce demand and supply (including indicators of workforce stress or ineffectiveness or unmet requirements for critical skills or leadership capabilities) are identified, as are actions to close these gaps. The costs and benefits of available approaches for filling these gaps, which may include additional recruiting,

---

[1] The dearth of literature on the topic could be due to the fact that few companies develop empirically driven workforce requirements standards or that these activities are sensitive or proprietary (indeed, two companies we spoke with declined to share their approaches for this reason).

retraining or training, and use of a contingent workforce, are assessed to determine the most effective approach. Organizations then monitor and adjust as necessary.

Unlike the public sector, private-sector competitive pressures motivate continuous reassessment of workforce requirements where responsiveness to change is enabled by agile recruitment and compensation processes, use of temporary or contingent workforces, employment at will, and much greater use of lateral entry. This entire process is closely linked to revenue and budget forecasts. Finally, industry workforces are not centrally managed. In our observations, individual business units do their own workforce planning (with input from the headquarters or corporate level), and it is the business units, not headquarters, that determine labor demand (County of Fairfax, Virginia, 2003, Manning, 2012, Nataraj et al., 2014; U.S. Office Personnel Management, 2011; Society for Human Resource Management, 2015).

Figure 3.1. Elements of the Workforce Planning Process

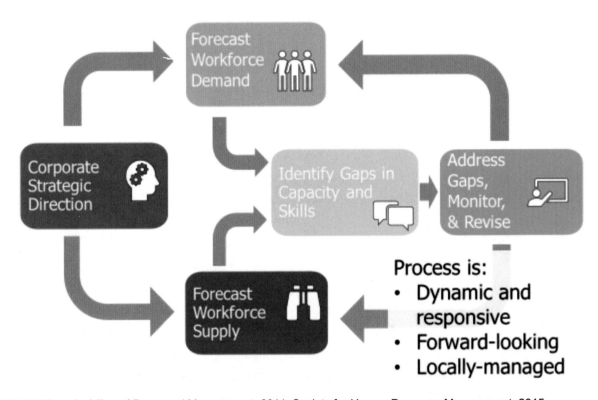

SOURCES: U.S. Office of Personnel Management, 2011; Society for Human Resource Management, 2015.

The workforce demand forecast (green box, Figure 3.1) is an estimate of the workforce size and skills mix needed in the future, as guided by the strategic plan. These assessments can be qualitative or quantitative, depending on the availability of data. Moreover, it is important to ensure that assumptions are clear and examined fully. High-volume, standardized tasks are more suited to quantitative modeling, and specialized or low-frequency tasks are more suited to qualitative techniques (such as expert opinion). (Cotten, 2007, pp. 16–17). According to Nataraj et al., 2014, workforce demand forecasting involves assessing

- workforce productivity and current workload
- expectations about future workload
- future workforce productivity.

Several approaches for determining workforce demand are discussed in the literature. These approaches are depicted in Figure 3.2, roughly in increasing order of the amount of resources (such as data and staff time) required to use the approach.

Figure 3.2. Methods Used for Determining Workforce Demand

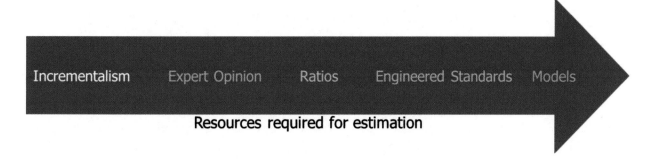

Incrementalism

Incrementalism uses existing workforce size as an indicator of future demand.[2] The incremental approach to developing demand estimates begins with the current workforce size and composition and makes adjustments on the margin for the organizational units that anticipate changes to workload drivers or worker productivity. For the most part, this approach assumes that year-to-year workforce demand will be relatively constant and that worker productivity remains unchanged. This approach has advantages in that the workforce demand remains relatively stable, it does not require extensive calculations; depending on how the approach is exercised, internal conflicts or competition for resources can be avoided. The disadvantages are that this approach does not provide incentives for innovative or labor-saving change, includes little guidance on how to make changes when they are necessary, and assumes that the work is conducted in the same way from year to year (Tucker, 1982; eFinanceManagement, 2018). We saw examples of this approach being used in local government and private industry.

---

[2] First introduced by Lindblom in 1959 as an approach to policy and public administration, incrementalism (Lindblom, 1959; Lindblom, 1979) has been applied in many contexts, including budgeting (which is closely linked to workforce planning). Critics note that the general concept can be difficult to define precisely, making it challenging to rigorously and empirically assess its usefulness (Berry, 1990).

Expert Opinion

Expert judgement develops estimates from the input of experienced individuals knowledgeable about the work that is conducted. Expert opinion can be gathered and synthesized in several ways—surveys, face-to-face discussions (using the nominal group technique), scenario analysis, or using the Delphi approach—each with its own advantages and potential biases. Expert judgement is the most common approach for forecasting workforce demand (Nataraj et al., 2014). (In Chapter 4, we discuss several problems related to the Air Force's use of expert opinion in developing ACS manpower standards that might benefit from more-sophisticated approaches.)

Ratios

Ratios relate demand drivers (often sales, output produced, or population served) to the number of workers. These drivers can be applied at an aggregate level or to various categories of workers without requiring a lot of data collection—specifically, only information on demand drivers and numbers of workers within each category of interest. However, the use of ratios to determine workforce demand assumes that worker productivity remains constant over the forecast period and for all levels of output. This may be a reasonable assumption for year-to-year forecasts or when productivity is expected to remain unchanged (unaffected by process change, workforce composition, economies of scale, or new technology, for example). Exemplars can be used as benchmarks when work centers are comparable and operated similarly (Nataraj et al., 2014).

Engineered Standards

Engineered standards are determined by measuring the time it takes for a trained worker to do a defined amount of work to a specified quality. They can be used to determine workforce demand but are also discussed in the research literature in the context of evaluating performance. Engineered standards discussed in the literature most commonly use examples from such activities as maintenance, manufacturing, and distribution and warehousing centers.

Modeling

Modeling approaches encompass both deterministic and probabilistic models (queuing models, simulation models, regression analyses). These approaches vary in the assumptions regarding productivity changes. The data requirements and resources required to develop and maintain these models are higher than for other approaches. For example, one modeling approach discussed with one company determines the optimal workforce levels using forecasts of workload factors (such as transactions) and service standards requirements to generate workload. Workload may be fixed, semivariable, or demand driven. Labor productivity standards for demand-driven workload are developed through time studies. Workforce requirements are built up by location and function. The predominant models that we came across in the literature are regression equations and simulations with imbedded queuing models. Much of Chapter 4 explores how the Air Force uses modeling to develop its ACS manpower standards.

Selecting an Approach

The approach or approaches an organization uses are generally determined by data availability, the required investment of time and resources to perform the analysis, the desired level of visibility into the reasons for a given staffing level, and the underlying relationship between workforce characteristics and key outputs that ultimately affect organizational performance measures (wait times, profit). Ultimately, workforce planning focuses on the workforce categories that significantly affect cost and revenue. Effective workforce planning employs a systems view of the workforce demand, supply, and business planning. It also incorporates measurement and monitoring in which information on the workload factors, time worked, and performance are recorded and incorporated in financial planning and short- and long-term workforce planning.

Practices We Observed

All organizations execute the processes illustrated in Figures 3.1 and 3.2 in some form. Table 3.1 lists the organizations we examined, along with key characteristics of how they execute these processes. We provide brief but complete descriptions of the processes used in these organizations to contrast them with Air Force approaches and to identify potentially adaptable practices. With the exceptions of the Army and Navy, we found no organization that develops manpower determinants comparable to those of the Air Force, most certainly not for the breadth of functions found in ACS. Many organizations develop workforce demand estimates as a step in their overall workforce planning process, in which workforce demand is typically determined by adjusting existing workforce levels for anticipated changes in strategy, mission, and operations (for example, when new technology is implemented) and then matched to supply estimates. Organizations with repetitive functions that have clear output measures often use quantitative models. The following subsections provide an overview of the approaches used by each of the examined organizations.

Table 3.1. Characteristics of Other Organizations' Manpower Practices

Organization	Responsible Office	Processes Used	Comments
U.S. Army	U.S. Army Manpower Analysis Agency (USAMAA)	Organization-specific manpower standards developed through common workload-measurement techniques	Applies to the Army generating force. Operating force requirements are determined by standard unit configurations.
U.S. Navy			
U.S. Fleet Forces Command (USFF)	Command Manpower Analysis Team (CMAT)	Organization-specific manpower requirements developed from mission, function, and task (MFT) documents	Applies to professional service activities, training functions, and headquarters services' activities. Each activity assessed is unique.
Commander, Navy Installations Command (CNIC)	Shore Manpower Optimization Team	Organization and function-oriented manpower requirement models developed from MFT documents and time audits	Process comparable to Air Force workshop process using automated tools for data collection and model application
Federal Bureau of Investigation (FBI)	Resource Planning Office (RPO), Resource Analysis Unit	Allocation of existing manpower into programs using threats and relative risks	While authorized billets are managed closely, allocation of these billets to locations is fairly stable.
Transportation Security Agency (TSA)	Workforce Management Division	Simulation model to determine number of screening lanes required to meet passenger and luggage waiting time standards	This applies to the front-line (passenger and luggage screening) workforce only; no formal methods are used for other workforces.
Fairfax County Government	Compensation and Workforce Analysis	Organization-specific manpower requirements developed from mission and occupational needs scaled for unit workload	Future needs are based on the current workforce and anticipated changes to mission and skill requirements.
Southern California Edison (SCE)		Corporatewide workforce planning process that incorporates strategic direction into workforce demand and supply planning, identifies gaps, develops actions to close the gaps, and monitors progress	
Walmart (literature only)		Bottom-up estimates, trend analyses, expert opinion, and engineered standards	Sales forecasts are drivers of workforce needs.
Health care sector (literature only)		Demand, service-level, and need-driven approaches; use of ratios of manpower to population or number of beds; some simulation and stochastic modeling (mostly specific functions or units)	Staffing requirements have multiple workload drivers and are critical to key performance measures (patient outcomes and financial).

NOTE: We spoke with two other private-sector organizations that declined to be identified for proprietary reasons.

U.S. Army Generating Force Requirements

USAMAA, within the Assistant Secretary of the Army Office of Manpower Requirements and Analysis (ASA[MR&A]), is responsible for developing an Army-wide manpower requirements determination method and for assisting ASA(MR&A) in ensuring the method is consistently applied. ASA(MR&A) has primary responsibility for overseeing the generating force manpower requirements development process.[3] Manpower requirements determination for the Army's generating force is distributed and is conducted at all levels—headquarters, Army major commands, and the installation. USAMAA is responsible for validating manpower studies and requirements developed by generating force commands; developing manpower requirements models for Headquarters, Department of the Army and generating force elements; and providing general manpower analysis support. Additionally, USAMAA provides manpower-related analysis for strategic initiatives and validates the manpower analysis conducted for concept plans.[4]

USAMAA undertakes six types of activities:

1. **Single-organization manpower studies to determine the minimum essential staffing requirements.** These studies, which are largely conducted by the organization with some USAMAA involvement, constituted much of the effort in the past.
2. **Modeling mathematically based requirements for specific functions across multiple organizations.** These models can take the form of manpower staffing ratios, equations, allocation rules, templates, etc., for performing specific functions (either within an organization or across organizations). Modeling work is coordinated among the Army major commands; Headquarters, Department of the Army functional managers; and USAMAA. These are the focus for future work.
3. **Strategic studies.** These take a comprehensive look at a function of interest because of observed organizational and process issues.
4. **Concept plans.** These are prepared when there are changes to organizational responsibilities and requirements; USAMAA reviews the manpower justifications used to modify the TDA.
5. **Effectiveness reviews.** These are used to assess an organization for potential improvement in manpower effectiveness and are advisory studies for information only. These studies use a *manpower relative value*, which is analogous to return on investment. The manpower relative value equals the benefit of the function divided by the cost of the function, where the benefit is the importance of the function as assessed by leadership, and the cost is the man-hours, man-years, or percentage of the organization's manpower required to execute the function.
6. **Reviews of standards that other Army organizations develop.**

Manpower requirements standards are developed by either USAMAA or the organization under study with USAMAA involvement using the approach depicted in Figure 3.3. According to AR 570-04, 2006, these models are to be reviewed every three years or more often if

---

[3] These requirements are known as tables of distribution and allowances (TDAs), although some generating forces may have operational duties. The Deputy Chief of Staff for Operations is responsible for the operating force requirements (Army Regulation [AR] 570-4, 2006). These requirements are known as modified tables of organization and equipment.

[4] According to AR 71-32, concept plans are detailed proposals to create or change one or more TDAs. The concept plan demonstrates that the changes support Army objectives and priorities and provides the organizational structure and workload-validated requirements for manpower and equipment (AR 71-32, 2019).

necessary (although we were told the USAMAA does not have the manpower staffs to consistently meet this requirement).[5]

Figure 3.3. Army Manpower Requirements Development Process

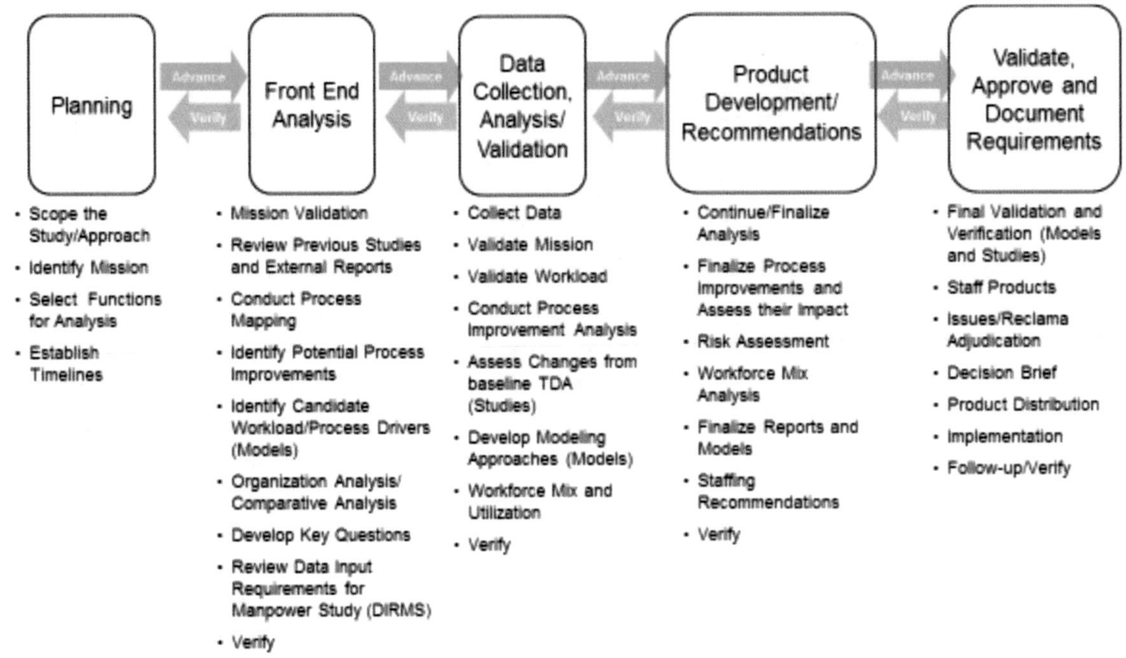

SOURCE: USAMAA, 2018.

Organizationally, the USAMAA has three interdisciplinary divisions (see Figure 3.4), which are aligned with the Army's force-generating commands. Each division chief is also a lead for an aspect of the analysis process: studies, models, and concept plans and in-sourcing. There are 30 GS-13 or higher billets for either operations researchers or management analysts and a few military billets.

Noteworthy Observations

USAMAA serves, in effect, as a method development, consultancy, and quality assurance organization. The organization under study does much of the requirements analysis and data collection, leveraging its own organic manpower capabilities, with USAMAA input throughout the process. USAMAA provides instructions, templates, standard operating procedures, and targeted training for conducting these studies. It also monitors each of the five study phases and verification steps to ensure that they are performed properly and can be validated. USAMAA

---

[5] The relevant regulation directs USAMAA to task major commands and direct reporting units to provide their three-year manpower study plans by June 30 and to redirect study efforts as necessary based on Army leadership priorities (AR 570-4, 2006).

must validate the completed studies before they can be implemented. Headquarters- or command-level interest, new work requirements, or the age of the existing standard (organizations with old standards may have trouble competing for manpower authorizations) may trigger studies. By Army regulation, these standards should be developed every two to five years, although some are older.

Figure 3.4. U.S. Army Manpower Analysis Agency Organization

SOURCE: USAMAA, 2018.
NOTES: FORSCOM = U.S. Army Forces Command; USARC = U.S. Army Reserve Command; MEDCOM = U.S. Army Medical Command; USAREUR = U.S. Army Europe; USASOC = U.S. Army Special Operations Command; HRC = Human Resources Command; USARAF = U.S. Army Africa; USARNORTH = U.S. Army North; USARSOUTH = U.S. Army South; TRADOC = U.S. Army Training and Doctrine Command; ARNG/NGB = Army National Guard/National Guard Bureau; ATEC = U.S. Army Test and Evaluation Command; INSCOM = U.S. Army Intelligence and Security Command; USARPAC = U.S. Army Pacific; USARCENT = U.S. Army Central; CIDC = U.S. Army Criminal Investigation Command; AMC = U.S. Army Materiel Command; IMCOM = U.S. Army Installation Management Command; USACE = U.S. Army Corps of Engineers; USAASC = U.S. Army Acquisition Support Center; MDW = Military District of Washington; USMA = U.S. Military Academy; SMDC = U.S. Army Space and Missile Defense Command; ARCYBER = U.S. Army Cyber Command; NETCOM = U.S. Army Network Enterprise Technology Command.

The Army's methods for these studies appear to be comparable to those of the Air Force, with the distinction that the Army develops standards focused on organizations more commonly than on functions. The Army is trying to move away from single-organization studies to develop more models, which can take the form of manpower staffing ratios, equations, allocation rules, simulations, etc. Models are "owned" by the organizations under study.

USAMAA has developed a data-gathering template and tool (a Microsoft Excel workbook) called Data Input Requirements for a Manpower Study (DIRMS) for organizing the process steps; identifying the legal, policy, and regulatory requirements; and gathering data on number of outputs, time, and backlogged essential mission work. The organization under study, with the assistance of USAMAA, identifies the major functions for each work center at the beginning of the study and inputs these functions, their outputs, annual counts, and data sources into the DIRMS. Time estimates for each employee in the work center are collected as a percentage of time spent on each of the functions, to be used in conjunction with an assumption that personnel will work 1,740 hours per year (regardless of whether he or she is military or civilian). During the study, this information may be validated through interviews, observation, and additional research. The workbook also includes overall instructions and guidance for identifying backlogged mission essential work and new workload for the mission and function. The organization under study collects data over a six- to 12-month period. Supporting documentation, such as organizational charts, statements of work, and process maps (should they exist), is also required.

As noted in Chapter 2, the Air Force's manpower development process includes a process improvement step, but we did not find that element in USAMAA's standard development. As with the Air Force, the Army process ensures that unnecessary work is not counted. That is, the work performed must be based on documented Army requirements; otherwise, tasks are eliminated, and standards are developed for the minimum required number of personnel. Experienced USAMAA analysts also understand the typical requirements for various functions and can apply this experience to provide ad hoc benchmarks to organizations that include common activities. However, these are not *process improvements* per se. Additionally, USAMAA has an effectiveness review analysis product. Conducted at the request of an organization for its own internal use, these reviews assess the relative cost per unit value produced by each activity and can lead to further performance improvement studies.

U.S. Navy Shore Manpower Requirements

The Navy has distinct processes for developing afloat and ashore manpower requirements, both of which are overseen by the Chief of Naval Operations (CNO), Total Force Requirements Division (N12). The Navy Manpower Analysis Center, which reports to CNO N12, develops manpower requirements for all afloat units, while Navy shore manpower requirements (for CNO staff, training schools, installation staff, history and heritage, depots, etc.) are the responsibility of budget-submitting offices and are managed by CNO N12.

Shore manpower requirements are based on the approved MFT documents for the activity.[6] Deputy CNO for Manpower, Personnel, Training, and Education approves the standards. Each shore activity requires an MFT document indicating missions the unit is expected to accomplish, functions to be performed to accomplish the mission, and tasks taken to meet policy directives or other approved taskings. In most cases, commands are responsible for documenting the MFTs for organizations under their administrative chain of command. In contrast with the afloat units, which have distinct, operational requirements as a basis for determining manpower requirements, MFTs are not as well defined or standardized across units. Peacetime shore manpower requirements are documented in a *statement of manpower requirements* (SMR), while wartime requirements are documented in a *mobilization SMR*. The distribution of the manpower into

---

[6] MFTs for shore activities are included in Office of the Chief of Naval Operations Instruction (OPNAVINST) 5440 and 5450 series can be found at DON, "Department of the Navy Issuances," website, undated.

position-level staffing requirements is recorded in the activity manpower document. The Total Force Manpower System is the information system with all the requirements for shore and deployable forces.

The two budget-submitting offices with the largest manpower requirements groups are USFF and Commander, Navy Installation Command.

Fleet Forces Command

USFF organizes, staffs, trains, maintains, and equips Navy forces and develops fleet readiness. In addition to Atlantic fleet afloat commands, its subordinate shore commands include Combined Joint Operations from the Sea Center of Excellence; Board of Inspection and Survey; Military Sealift Command; Naval Meteorology and Oceanography Command; Naval Warfare Development Command; Naval Information Forces; Tactical Training Group, Atlantic; and Navy Munitions Command, Atlantic.[7] USFF CMAT comprises approximately 26 civilians in management and program-analysis positions in the GS-0343 series (at the levels of GS-9/11/12s). Team leads are usually GS-13s, and the director is a GS-14.

CMAT is responsible for between 60,000 to 70,000 billets in maintenance, training, and staff functions that are filled with civilian, military, and contractor personnel. Although the shore commands may have similar functions, such as training, each of these commands has its own operational cycles, maintenance availabilities, and training requirements that affect organizational size and structure. Therefore, these constitute unique organizations, with functions blended in different ways. This precludes development of functional standards, so the manpower requirements determinations for each organization are unique.

The manpower analysis team develops a manpower requirement using the activities identified in MFT documents. Each command prepares MFT documents. CMAT supplements them, as needed, with Office of the Secretary of Defense instructions, White House directives, or National Defense Authorization Act requirements. While CMAT may use additional information to supplement MFT documents, CMAT personnel do not modify these documents. CMAT interviews department heads, work center supervisors, and other select personnel to develop performance work statements (PWSs) for the major activities that are performed weekly. CMAT personnel do not discuss every task and rarely develop process maps unless there is a problem. Each task has technical time estimates made by experienced CMAT staff and validated by the individuals responsible for the work. Indirect work is considered part of normal duty requirements and is included in these requirements. While MFT documents do not contain programmable factors that drive workload, CMAT is developing some predictive tools to provide guidance for how workload may vary.

---

[7] See OPNAVINST 5440.77B, 2012.

CMAT follows these steps to produce an SMR:

- **Planning:** Review the MFT documents, draft a PWS, and establish a manpower baseline. Leadership involvement is key to success.
- **Data collection and analysis:** Collect previous studies, directives, and records; conduct an organizational analysis (which can include comparing similar activities and look for process improvement); refine the PWS and identify workload indicators; and measure work. Workload is measured by reviewing specific directives, CNO-approved staffing standards, position staffing, or direct time measurements and through operational audits, personal interviews, and technical estimates.
- **Document and present results:** Develop the draft SMR, present the results to the activity for review (30-day limit on review period), resolve reclama issues, seek USFF N1 approval, and finalize the SMR.

The budget-submitting office uses the SMR to support budget actions and activity manpower document changes. The normal cycle between requirements reviews normally occur every eight to nine years, but the CMAT reviews billet changes annually. CMAT does not conduct normal process improvement (the inspector general performs this role) but does provide informal benchmarks to the function, when possible. In general, the Navy shore manpower requirements determination process USFF uses is less quantitative and rigorous than the Air Force's approaches.

Naval Installations Command

CNIC is responsible for organizing, manning, training, maintaining, and equipping Navy base operating support functions and infrastructure consistently, effectively, and efficiently for all shore installation services and support functions to the fleet (OPNAVINST 5450.339, 2011). The CNIC manpower office, with five personnel, uses a four-step process to develop the SMR. Some of these steps have been automated to leverage the limited staff and to increase installation participation:

- **Perform background research and hold a planning workshop with the functional representatives.** If a baseline PWS is available, manpower personnel will use it, but organizations and processes change, and the PWS is often not maintained. As a result, personnel generally begin with the MFT documents, instructions, and any guidance documents to pull together a strawman PWS for the functionals to refine. This also ensures that the functionals own the PWS and that manpower requirements are developed from accurate and vetted PWSs. The goal of the workshop is to define the mission of the function, complete a PWS, develop a measurement plan, coordinate a schedule for gathering and reporting measurements, and get buy-in on the process. Unless there is a lot of functional churn or a request for an in-person workshop, these workshops are held virtually. Our interviewee's opinion is that an in-person workshop can be advantageous because it is possible to get a better sense of uncertainties and where there is agreement, but the virtual workshop streamlines the process and facilitates greater participation.
- **Collect measurement data using an electronic data capture tool that is sent to a representative sample of installations.** The data tool is an Excel workbook that contains

task descriptions and input fields for frequency, time required, and skill level. These fields may have drop-down menus and other features that guide the input and provide opportunities for explanation (see Figure 3.5 for an example of an input sheet and example instruction). The intent is to have someone who is well versed in the process, such as someone who actually does the work, enter values into the data capture tool; this person is not necessarily a supervisor because the estimate should represent the average time a fully qualified person should take to perform the task. Sometimes, respondents at a given location will pull together a committee to complete the data. Other worksheets in the workbook collect information on workload indicators and current manning.

- **Assess and analyze data, including understanding outliers and cleaning up discrepancies.** An activity that occurs at a limited number of locations may be considered a variance and removed from the model.

- **Develop the manpower model using data and workload indicators.** Quantitative workload indicators are preferred and must be available at all locations. When possible, these models are regression equations but may be simple factors or averages. Once the PWS is stable, the man-hours available are distributed among grade and skill levels for the SMR (this is done in a separate meeting that focuses on the minimum skills required to do the job).

**Figure 3.5. Commander, Navy Installations Command
Data Capture Tool—Task, Frequency, and Time Worksheet**

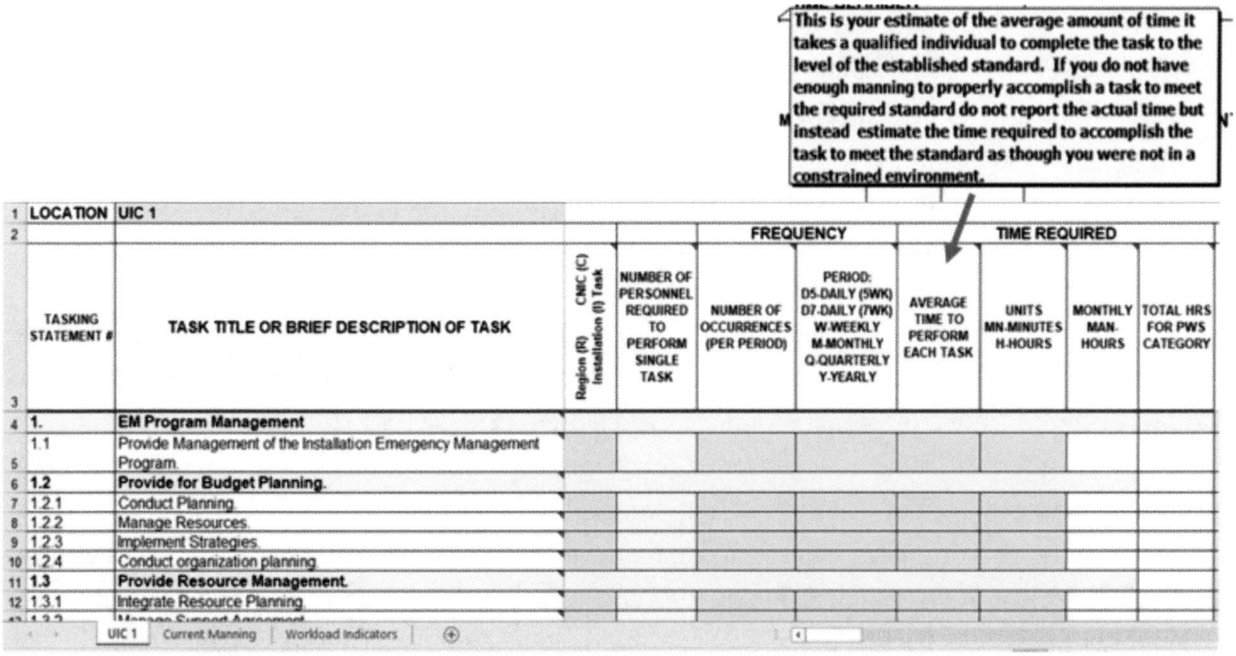

NOTE: Each column heading is explained in a pop-up that appears when the cursor is on the cell. For example, the guidance provided for the Average Time to Perform Each Task is shown in the call-out box and blue arrow in the figure. Note also that the data capture tool contains input sheets for current manning and workload indicators (bottom left of the figure).

A normal study takes three to four months, unless there is a lot of complexity or unless a large number of functions are involved. The Navy Manpower Analysis Center is not involved in the model development process but does review the study and archive the model.

The manpower office has also developed a manpower application tool that it shares with the regions and the installations. This automated tool allows the region and installations to apply the new standard to each location. The tool generates the new total manpower requirements distributed into the grade and skill table for a workload indicator and compares the new requirement to current funded billets in terms of manpower and budget for each installation in the region.

Process Improvement

Formal process improvement is not incorporated into manpower requirements development because the manpower office does not control the process. When the PWS is created, functional representatives will discuss best practices, but it is up to the representatives to enforce best practices at the installations. Ultimately the process is controlled by the functional managers and process changes are implemented through headquarters and regional offices.

Federal Bureau of Investigation

The FBI has approximately 35,000 personnel, more than 13,000 of whom are special agents; another 3,000 are intelligence analysts; and nearly 19,000 are professional staff. The total annual funding is around $12.5 billion (Office of the Inspector General, Department of Justice, 2017). About two-thirds of the FBI workforce is located in the field, which comprises 56 field offices, roughly 400 satellite offices, four specialized field installations, and 23 foreign liaison posts. The investigative arm of the FBI is organized into seven programs: applicant matters, civil rights, counterterrorism, foreign counterintelligence, organized crime and drugs, violent crimes and major offenders, and financial crime (FBI, 2014).

RPO conducts manpower analyses and reports directly to an associate deputy director. This office has business management expertise and conducts analyses that inform the distribution of the workforce among the seven programs, which are located across 56 field offices and other smaller locations. This office analyzes and manages the funded staff level (FSL), which is the total number of positions that the FBI's appropriations cover. In the current budgetary environment, this office has been focusing on developing models that allow it to closely manage the FSL, which involves understanding the consequences of congressional authorizations on the number of positions the FBI could expect to fund (adjusted for year-to-year changes to compensation and grade structure) and predicting the hiring process (in terms of time to onboard and likelihood of completion). The FSL is expected to remain stable overall in the foreseeable future; for the last several years, the FBI has been staffed at 97 to 98 percent of FSL.

Staffing needs for the field offices are determined using a three-step, top-down approach beginning with the total FSL and an assessment of national risks for each of the program areas.

Risk indicators for each of the programs are used to calculate the relative risk in each geographic area. This relative risk and several other factors are used to distribute positions in the FSL to the programs and to the field offices (this process works best when resources are increasing, otherwise there are not many opportunities to shift positions from one field office to another).[8] Since FBI work is complex and varies with the program and the type of investigation, RPO does not build process-oriented descriptions for allocating or determining the needed FSL.

Within a field office, funded staff positions are distributed among the programs at the local level either by the assistant director in charge (for the larger locations) or the special agent in charge using an assessment of the threats in that area and a determination of the associated workload for that particular threat.[9] (Some threats generate more workload than others; for example, criminal threats are more labor-intensive than cyber and other threats.) The special agent in charge develops a plan annually for allocating his or her agent positions and submits it to headquarters for review and approval. Headquarters occasionally modifies these plans to reconcile national priorities and local priorities. The special agent in charge also has the authority to surge in a particular line of effort and reallocate resources accordingly. Individual special agents are expected to work across programs to maintain flexibility. Other staffing needs, such as for administrative support or operations specialists, are built from the number of agents needed.[10] In the past, other staff needs were determined using ratios developed from studies of the way people work. These studies were, however, conducted more than a decade ago; some of the job codes no longer exist and are no longer routinely used. The current focus is on distributing these personnel resources equitably, and ratios may be calculated for this purpose.

The FBI has a system for tracking work performed that is used for reporting to Congress and for informing the threat review process: the Time Utilization and Recordkeeping system. Information on time spent on cases (by type, not a specific investigation) is input every two weeks for select job series involved in field work (for example, special agents, intelligence positions, computer science positions, foreign language translators, and forensic accountants). This information is not routinely audited for accuracy; while there are codes for indirect work, this system does not generally capture small, one-time tasks. Field offices use this information to manage their personnel, and FBI Headquarters uses it for planning or reviewing how programs are spending resources.

---

[8] RPO considers a total of about 13 factors when advising on how to allocate FSL. These factors include time utilization data, facilities, leadership, and performance.

[9] In fiscal year (FY) 2013, the FBI developed a threat review and prioritization process in which field offices identify and prioritize threats annually. Field offices use the threat bands (the bands indicate national threats and local threat priorities) that emerge from this process to establish mitigation strategies and to allocate resources. This process also provides a common planning framework so that FBI headquarters has the ability to look for gaps and resource issues across field offices, although it has been criticized for its focus on known threats, as opposed to emerging ones (Hoffman, Meese, and Roemer, 2015).

[10] *Operations specialists* are individuals who perform tactical-level analysis, for example, reviewing bank account activity.

Process improvement is integral to all analyses in the RPO. However, another unit, the Business Process Management Unit, typically conducts in-depth process improvement studies, although the RPO may perform targeted improvement studies on an ad hoc basis or by request (this often occurs when a function is asking for additional resources).

Transportation Security Agency Resource Allocation

TSA's Workforce Management Division is responsible for determining the labor requirements at 450 airports. The division estimates workforce demand for frontline personnel using its proprietary Enhanced Staffing Model. TSA's approach is most applicable to Air Force functions that have predictable, repetitive activities with good information on the determinants, comparable to the way the Air Force's LCOM model handles logistics functions.

The Enhanced Staffing Model is a discrete simulation model that calculates the number of screening lanes required to meet passenger wait-time standards. Only the front-line workforce (passenger and luggage screening) is modeled; there are no formal methods for estimating other workforces.

The model generates workforce demand using inputs on

- airport profiles
- flight-driven work demand for passenger and baggage screening
- productivity rates and standards
- optimized schedule standards.

The airport scheduling officer inputs airport profile information—the number of concourses, bag zones, checkpoints, equipment, etc., in addition to airline and flight information. These airport personnel also have the ability to enter exceptions when facilities have physical characteristics that affect the number of lanes (about 100 airports) or when airline policies or flight characteristics suggest the amount of baggage will be different from what normally can be expected (about 80 airports). Passenger volume is projected using the highest average daily volume for a 28-day period within the previous year (excluding the three highest and lowest days). Screening productivity rates and standards, determined by the Office of Requirements and Capability Analysis Division using time studies, are applied to determine the number of screening lanes needed to maintain wait times under ten minutes (five minutes for precheck). Standards are developed and reviewed annually for passenger throughput rates by lane type and equipment, staffing requirements for passenger screening by lane type and function, baggage throughput by bag size and equipment, staffing requirements for baggage screening by equipment type, among others. The model produces an optimized schedule for the required workforce.

Model outputs are adjusted for staff requirements that are not captured in the model. These include training time, paid time off, overtime, supervisory ratios, and risk-based demand for additional security. For example, supervisory ratios vary with the size of the airport, being between 1:10 and 1:12 supervisors to staff, depending on the number of checkpoints. Overtime is nominally programmed in at 3 percent to account for flight delays (larger airports tend to get more, smaller airports less). Because managers at each airport establish their own shift schedules, the optimized schedule is not always used. The Workforce Management Division personnel assess the variance, or efficiency, of the existing schedule from the optimized schedule and use this information to adjust allowances for training or paid time off, the assumption being that those with lulls in the schedule can use that time for training and leave and would therefore not need as great an adjustment.

Seasonality in demand also affects the application of the model outputs. Airports that have large fluctuations between busy and nonbusy periods are considered seasonal airports. Passenger volume is analyzed, and staffing is set somewhat below the model outputs, with the assumption that a part-time or on-call workforce will be used during the peak periods, and training will be conducted during the lulls.[11] Staffing determinations are made months before the peak season so that airports have time to prepare.

Budget forecasting is challenging. While workforce staffing is determined bottom up, budget projections are prepared at a high level two years in advance using aggregate ratios of staff to volume. If the budget forecast does not match the bottom-up staffing determinations, some of the requirements may be met by reducing training time.

The model is also used to anticipate how changes to screening practices and services affect workforce demand.

Fairfax County Government

Fairfax County government is organized into 53 agencies to serve more than 1.1 million residents and nearly 186,000 schoolchildren (County of Fairfax, Virginia, 2017). Table 3.2 lists the number of county employees by function.

In Fairfax County, the Human Resources Department guides workforce planning in conjunction with the Department of Management and Budget. The workforce planning process is intended to ensure that the workforce is adequately sized and includes the requisite skills to effectively and efficiently conduct county business into the future. One step in the planning process estimates workforce demand. However, Fairfax County does not develop formal workforce requirements standards as part of this analysis.

---

[11] TSA has both a part-time and a national deployment force that can be used to staff to peak demands.

Table 3.2. Full-Time Equivalent Fairfax County Government Employees, by Function

Function	Number of Employees in Fiscal Year 2017
Primary government	
General government administration	2,259
Judicial administration	401
Public safety	4,459
Public works	566
Health and welfare	3,508
Community development	528
Parks, recreation, and cultural	717
Subtotal	12,438
Component units	
Public Schools	24,688
Redevelopment and Housing Authority	226
Park Authority	575
Subtotal	25,489
Total employees	37,927

SOURCE: County of Fairfax, Virginia, 2017, p. 290.

The Human Resources Department works with the agencies on all their workforce planning needs and workforce administration. Workforce planning is conducted biannually, when the Human Resources Department and the Department of Management and Budget meet with each agency and the agency's human resources staff. The focus of workforce planning is to ensure that the agency has the requisite number of personnel with the needed skills. This process includes reviewing the purposes of the agency and the business functions it conducts for the county and identifying what is changing in terms of mission function, strategies, technologies, and desired performance levels. These trends and changes from current practices, in turn, determine the positions that are needed and whether or not new job classifications and occupational groups are necessary.

The size of the workforce is determined during the budgeting process. Each division will have its own set of workload drivers. Transportation, for example, looks at the number and size of projects anticipated, and Fire and Rescue considers call volume and response time. When a new unit is created, rules of thumb and analogous units are used to determine workforce needs. In general, there is little opportunity to increase the number of county employees, and the county does not have a formula for determining workforce requirements. There must be a compelling business case for adding positions (a new mission or activity that has strong political support and that has some identified revenue sources); workforce reductions, for the most part, are accomplished through natural attrition.

Southern California Edison

SCE, a subsidiary of Edison International, provides electricity to much of Southern California. Edison International has approximately 12,500 full-time employees (Edison International, 2018).

The utility industry is responding to the effects of deregulation on business strategy, needed investments in aging infrastructure while maintaining a rate structure, and anticipated large numbers of retirements, which in turn has led to changes in workforce planning (Edison International, 2018). SCE is moving away from a predominately bottom-up project-focused process that generates billets (which are balanced with available budget) to a strategic focus that involves forecasting workforce supply—by month, job title, and position—for each operational unit, while at the same time assessing strategic priorities to anticipate future workforce needs (skills and numbers).

Prior to 2011, workforce planning was not standardized across the operational units. At that time, operational units generated information on the workforce at irregular times using different workforce definitions and data, precluding the ability to plan corporatewide. Moreover, workforce forecasts were often based on near-term activities and not strategic objectives. Beginning in 2011, SCE developed a common workforce planning process for all the operational units that included standardizing the workforce information requested; modeling retirement and attrition corporatewide; and coordinating workforce planning with other business processes, such as finance and facilities planning. One of the benefits of the new workforce planning system is linking workforce budget planning to workforce demand forecasting, so that budget and headcount are consistent with each other (Manning, 2012).

Strategic workforce planning is still fairly new and immature at SCE, and the human resources department is developing the foundational pieces for strategic workforce planning, which includes developing relationships with the operational units, implementing software systems and models, and leveraging existing data sources. The common workforce drivers are numbers of customers and revenue, and the existing workforce is used as the baseline for a five-year forecast. The forecast begins with the current workforce headcount and adds recruiting goals for existing vacancies and additional positions that are needed, as determined by business decisions and forecasts of workforce drivers. Losses that are due to forecasted attrition and redeployments are subtracted to get a headcount for the end of the planning period.

There are 18 to 20 operational units, including functionally oriented units, such as transmission and distribution lines (the largest unit with roughly 7,000 employees); customer support units, such as call center and business customer support; and staff units, such as finance, information technology, human resources, and strategy. As of this writing, only the two largest operational units, transmission and distribution and customer support, have their own human resources personnel that do workforce planning.

As it transitions to strategic workforce planning, SCE has maintained a hybrid approach. The transmission and distribution unit still has the artifacts of approaches used when the industry was more regulated, and the business call center, the second largest operational unit, engages with SCE corporate headquarters on strategically driven workforce planning. The transmission and distribution unit employs a billet management philosophy, which looks at skills needed for a particular project and builds up workforce demand from forecasts of the numbers and size of projects. The number of billets is forecast using the volume of capital projects, historical patterns, and budget expectations. If the number of billets is underestimated, a contingent workforce is used. The transmission and distribution unit has its own staffing group that works with the corporate headquarters workforce planning group. However, because this operational unit has a unique function, it operates somewhat independently.

In contrast, the business customer call center works more closely with corporate headquarters and uses more-typical workforce management practices. The call center forecasts a workload driver to determine workforce demand—in this case, call volume—using a commercially available software tool. Anticipated workforce demand is then compared with forecasted supply. Supply gaps can be addressed either through employee development, external sources or temporary help, reassignments, or outsourcing (SCE planners refer to these options as build, buy, redeploy, or outsource).

In sum, the corporate human resources department focuses on industry trends, corporate strategy, and ways of becoming more efficient to determine what skills and capabilities are needed in the workforce and how to develop this workforce. The operational units focus on managing the existing workforce, determining needs and demand, and continuous process improvement (for which the units have primary responsibility and are motivated by saving costs and pressures from market trends). Each of the units is responsible for managing its workforces and for using the approach that fits its operating environment. However, the corporate human resources department is implementing a corporatewide approach to strategic workforce planning and, as of this writing, is focusing on identifying the data systems and needs of the operational units.

Walmart

Walmart has on the order of 2.4 million employees and uses workforce planning, as others do, to ensure that workforce needs can be met with workforce supply.[12] According to open-source literature, Walmart planners determine workforce needs from forecasts of consumer demand and sales in three ways: bottom-up analysis, trend (top-down) analysis, and expert

---

[12] Our efforts to arrange a discussion with Walmart personnel were unsuccessful. This discussion is based solely on open-source information.

opinion. The *bottom-up analysis* begins with a forecast of demand for front-line employees and builds demand for each tier in the organizational structure off these estimates of workforce need. The second, *trend analysis*, forecasts future need using current changes and needs. For example, Walmart analyzes recent human resource trends (such as increasing demand in a skill area) and uses this information to extrapolate future workforce needs. The third method, *expert opinion* uses the Delphi method to forecast future human resources needs using a structured elicitation of expert opinion. Walmart may use this approach when adding new stores or product lines. In this case human resources experts estimate the workforce requirements, including the number of employees needed for each job type (for example, supply chain management, inventory control and management, or sales jobs, etc.) using the Delphi method (Thompson, 2017, p. 1).[13] Sales are an indicator of workforce needs. As sales forecasts change, Walmart adjusts the workforce supply in several ways—either through recruiting practices, compensation policies, or by hiring temporary workers for short term needs (Thompson, 2017).

Health Care Sector

The health care industry, as a whole, is quite complex, and many modeling approaches have been developed and applied to countries, health care facilities, specific medical units, and cadres of workers to determine the appropriate workforce size. Some limitations to using these approaches include data requirements that cannot be readily met, the need for operational expertise to describe standard processes and to delineate activities to be modeled, and the necessary stakeholder and management involvement and buy-in. As a result, heavy reliance on ratios appears to continue, modified to varying degrees by panels of experts who use their judgement to account for complex staffing decisions affected by patient characteristics, facility physical characteristics, and effective mixes of workforce skills. We also found approaches whose workforce requirements were driven by either level of service desired, health care needs for maintaining a health population, or health services demanded (used) by the population (Sharma et al., 2014; Dreesch et al., 2005).

The health care sector as a whole does not have a clearly superior approach for estimating workforce needs. But some of the methods developed for specific functions may inform Air Force approaches by suggesting improved models and data-collection techniques and in understanding the technical and management challenges of applying these approaches. We highlight several here.

---

[13] Searches on LinkedIn suggest that Walmart also develops engineered standards, primarily for logistics and warehousing functions, but because there was no publicly available information and because requests for interviews were not granted, we do not have details on this activity.

World Health Organization's Workload Indicators of Staffing Need

The World Health Organization's Workload Indicators of Staffing Need (WISN) is a prominent demand-based method used to determine staffing requirements for health care facilities in international contexts. Developed in the 1980s, WISN improves on traditionally used aggregate ratios, such as population-to-staff ratios (e.g., number of nurses or doctors per capita) and facility-based staffing ratios (e.g., number of nurses and number of doctors for a health care facility). Ratios, while fairly simple to compute, do not account for variability in the demand for services and the actual workload. In contrast, the WISN method develops staffing requirements based on patient needs and observed workload.

The WISN approach is comparable to the Air Force's methods and entails identifying the activities (at the appropriate level of detail), developing time estimates (referred to as *activity standards*), and applying estimates of workload factors (health care utilization) to determine the workload for each activity and cadre (worker type). As in other applications, activity times can be determined using standard general approaches—direct measurement, timekeeping, survey, interviews, or expert judgement. Before the workforce requirement is calculated, the total available staff time (analogous to the Air Forces' MAF) needs to be determined; these factors can then be combined to determine the workforce requirement. The WISN method can be applied to a facility, a region, or a class of health care worker. The computed workforce requirement is compared to the actual workforce size to indicate surpluses and shortages for a cadre at a facility (or region), while the ratio of the actual to the required number of staff is a measure of the workload pressure on the existing staff (World Health Organization, 2010).

When the WISN approach was piloted in public-sector hospitals in Turkey, it became apparent that the use of expert panels was most successful if the panel members had a certain level of authority and relevant experience. In addition, defining activities at the right level of detail using the panel approach is nontrivial because there is a tendency for panels to work at too detailed a level to be practicable. Additionally, the WISN approach in general will have more acceptance if facility managers understand the technique, so stakeholder involvement is helpful. Moreover, workload estimates could be skewed if another resource (other than staff) is underresourced; therefore, any staff requirement should be revisited if additional resources become available. Because of the breadth and complexity of health care service provision, this approach was recommended for health care facilities that have relatively simple operating structures (Ozcan, 1999).

Nurse Cadre Staff Requirements

Nurse staff requirements are of special interest because nurses represent the largest proportion of hospital operating costs and because adequate staffing directly effects patient outcomes (Agency for Healthcare Research and Quality, 2018). The demand for nurses changes by shift; patient condition, acuity, and turnover; the availability of support staff; and the skill mix, among other factors. In practice, nursing workforce size is determined in a number of ways,[14] but surveys indicate that there is a continual need to improve on these methods. The models are of two general types:

- **Fixed staffing models** use fixed mandated staffing ratios that require a set number of nurses for a particular unit, shift, or nurse-to-patient ratio. This approach clearly does not closely relate staffing to actual workload.
- **Flexible staffing models** adjust the number of nurses and the nurse-to-patient ratio according to such workload factors as patient condition and acuity, the physical layout of the nursing unit, or patient census (Avalere Health LLC, 2015).

One study used multiple methods for determining nursing activity times in surgical, internal medicine, and elder-care wards in a hospital setting. First, a two-round Delphi technique was used to develop consistent and measurable definitions of nursing activities in these wards (102 activities were identified, which is approximately one-half of all the nursing activities in these units). Second, activity times were measured over a six-month period in one of three ways: direct observation by third parties (13,292 observations) using work sampling techniques, self-reported direct time measurement (3,000 observations), and subjective assessment by nursing staff—with the selection of measurement approach based on criteria associated with the frequency with which the activities are performed and the ability to unambiguously measure the activity. Third, the measured times were reviewed by nursing experts; in nearly all cases, the subjective judgement of the nursing experts increased the measured time estimate (Myny et al., 2010).

Operation Research Methods

There is also a large literature on applying mathematical models to various facets of hospital operations, such as patient demand forecasting, scheduling and rostering staff, and financial planning, but there is little evidence these methods are routinely used for determining workforce size. We found a couple of instances of operations research methods being *developed* for determining staff size, but it is unclear how frequently, if at all, these approaches are *used*. For example, a discrete-event simulation model (using the nurse protocol applied to stochastically derived patients) coupled with a queuing model (of patient flow) was developed to determine the optimum required nurse staffing levels for perianesthesia care units (units that care for patients pre- and postanesthesia). Researchers found the previous method of applying ratios to the patient census underestimated the staffing needs by up to 20 percent relative to the simulation with queuing (Siddiqui, Morse, and Levin, 2017). In another example, a discrete-time Markov chain

---

[14] Because of safety and quality issues, some states and accreditation organizations require minimum staffing levels or prescribe general procedures. While there is no federal nurse staffing law (Avalere Health LLC, 2015, p. 20), Code of Federal Regulations, Title 42, §482.23(b), 2019, requires Medicare-eligible hospitals to have "adequate numbers of licensed registered nurses, licensed practical (vocational) nurses, and other personnel to provide nursing care to all patients as needed." At the state level, 15 states have laws that regulate nursing staffing practices (Oncology Nursing Society, undated). These states use one of three approaches: require hospitals to have staffing committees composed of nurses to ensure that staffing plans are adequate, mandate specific nurse-to-patient ratios by unit or specialty, or require facilities to provide staffing plans to the public and/or a regulatory body.

model, which estimates service process and transient patient inventory, was developed for an inpatient unit to match staffing with demand. When applied to a hospital, the model indicated that improved discharge practices can improve patient throughput and decrease the size of the premium staffing pool (Broyles, Cochran, and Montgomery, 2011). Abe et al., 2016c, states that, in publications from 2010 to January 2015,

> the most commonly used OR [operations research] methods were discrete event simulation and deterministic modeling (optimization), while the most common hospital operational areas where OR methods were applied were staff, room, and patient scheduling, as well as general patient flow assessment.[15]

Summary

The literature review and the vignettes of approaches that other government agencies and private industry use illustrate that, while we could not find evidence that the private sector develops "manning documents," commonly used methodologies for determining workforce demand are comparable to what the Air Force already uses, and function-to-function comparisons may provide benchmarks. There are, however, significant differences in how workforce demand is determined enterprisewide. In particular, industry's competitive pressures and profit motive provide important feedback loops and incentives for maintaining effective workforce sizes.[16] These pressures motivate continuous reassessment of workforce requirements, and the private sector has more flexibility to manage workforces (such as hiring temporary or contract workforces or agile recruitment and compensation processes) than the military does. In the private sector, workforce size is determined as a part of a larger business case analysis of locally determined priorities during budgeting processes. The private sector, because it does not have the same requirements for transparency as public agencies, offers limited insights for the Air Force into transferable, enterprisewide approaches for determining manpower requirements.

On the other hand, while their organizational structures are different, the Army and Navy approaches for generating force and shore-based requirements, respectively, have elements that may be useful for the Air Force to consider. For example, USAMAA operates as a professionalized consultancy to the organizations under study, which are responsible for developing their manpower standard according to the guidelines from USAMAA. In doing so the agency provides methodological guidance and oversight while leveraging its staff. USAMAA also deploys a data-collection tool, which is an Excel workbook the organization under study uses to facilitate the collection of workload indicators, the relative time spent on tasks, and

---

[15] Abe et al., 2016b, makes a similar statement about publications from the period of 1990 to 2009. See also Abe et al., 2016a.

[16] Economic theory holds that firms will produce up to the point that the marginal cost of production equals the marginal revenue. Workforce demand therefore depends on productivity, the cost of labor compared to other production inputs, and the demand for a firm's product, all of which change for various levels of output and over time. Therefore, in the private sector, effective workforce planning is dynamic, requiring feedback loops.

backlogged essential mission work, providing six to 12 months of information on which to base the requirements analysis. Outside USAMAA, the Army major commands and activities possess their own manpower experts who perform studies and may submit their reports to USAMAA for review.

The Navy's CNIC manpower group uses approaches for determining manpower requirements that are comparable to Air Force approaches but has chosen to deploy its tools via virtual and automated means for work data capture, analysis, and implementation. These tools streamline the manpower requirements determination process and provide additional information that can be used to improve both the development and the application of manpower standards. These have advantages in that virtual workshops can make it less costly and easier for locations to participate but still provide an opportunity to create buy-in for the study, develop or refine the PWS, and establish a data-gathering strategy. In addition, the data-capture tool the CNIC manpower group has developed allows local SMEs to provide potentially less-biased and more-consistent data (data guidelines are consistently presented, and observations are less likely to be distorted through the group dynamics typically found in a workshop setting) and additional descriptive material or explanations for unique locational circumstances. The analyst benefits from having a structured data set and the opportunity to reconcile outliers and understand drivers of variability. Moreover, the tool provides an auditable trail of responses and incentives for locations to provide the most accurate data available.

4. Processes for Developing Man-Hour Estimates

In this chapter, we examine the process for estimating required manpower for ACS functions. Multiple modeling techniques may be employed to determine required manpower, depending on the circumstances of a particular job or need. For certain positions, computing required manpower is straightforward; for example, the fixed number of security posts at a given location plus the training currencies required are the primary drivers of the Security Forces manpower needed to man those posts. When the manpower need is not fixed or constant, the anticipated need is estimated, a process that involves the historical frequency of the work performed, the time it takes to complete that work, and indicators of anticipated future work. In this chapter, we focus on the case in which manpower needs must be estimated in addressing the required work of an entire function across the entire Air Force.

Functional manpower needs are reviewed and estimated through a formal study. Study nominations may originate from Air Force major commands (MAJCOMs), air staff, or functional leadership. AFMAA develops and manages a study schedule, assigning studies to one of three MRSs. The study nomination process provides flexibility in establishing priorities for studying potentially undermanned functions; however, the lack of a systematic review of all functions opens the possibility of missed opportunities to reallocate manpower resources from more generously manned functions.

Within the MRS, a study lead directs and executes the study from start to finish. The study lead is typically either a midgrade civilian or a senior enlisted airman. Most commonly, the study lead does not have technical expertise in the function being studied. We note, however, that functionally or MAJCOM-aligned portfolios of studies are assigned to specific MRSs, with the presumption that these MRSs develop experience and rapport over time with specific stakeholders and mission sets. MRS flight chiefs manage the study leads, and additional MRS staff may assist the study lead as needed.

The scope of work for individual studies is captured in a project charter. Studies contain three major phases leading to a determination of the required manpower. In the first phase, familiarization, the study lead defines the essential work of the function, culminating in a process map for each process the function performs. In the second phase, SMEs are engaged during workshops to verify the process maps, provide time estimates, identify resources that can provide process frequencies, and review processes for potential improvement.[1] In the third phase,

---

[1] Workshops are the current tool of choice for addressing these elements. Alternatives are available and may be used less frequently in certain circumstances (e.g., a study of smaller scope). Here, we are focusing on the primary tool for function-wide studies. Field measurement, a more traditional tool, is an alternative but is expected to be an exception to the common choice of workshops (AFMAN 38-208 Vol. I, 2007, pp. 65–70).

standards are developed using the inputs from the SMEs. The following sections describe each of these phases.

Familiarization

Critical inputs for estimating required manpower for a function at a given location include the time it takes to complete required work and the frequency with which work is executed. A function may execute dozens of individual units of work, termed *processes*, and each process may consist of multiple tasks that must be executed to complete the process.[2] The processes and tasks must be well defined before process time and frequency can be used to determine manpower need. The final goal of this phase of the study is to produce a process map for each function that clearly defines the unit of work and each component task.

The MRS study lead develops process maps with guidance from functional representatives. As we noted earlier, the study lead typically does not have personal experience in the particular function being studied. Therefore, before building the process maps, the lead must develop expertise in the function's work responsibilities. The lead begins by examining all available information about the function—organizational policy and guidance, organization charts, publications, mission essential task lists, unit manpower documents, training material, position descriptions, management information systems, performance measures in use, and other relevant documentation (AFMAN 38-102, 2019, pp. 19–20). The lead also reviews prior manpower studies when available; however, final reports of prior studies have historically tended to contain the resulting manpower standards but not the input information leading up to that standard that would be highly valuable for a new study.[3]

In addition to a thorough examination of all available documentation, the MRS study lead interviews functional leadership. Accompanied by functional representatives, the lead then visits multiple bases to observe the work performed and to gain direct feedback from those carrying out the function's processes. Armed with primary information gathered from the functional leadership and site visits and the available documentation, the lead then produces a draft process map for each process for which the function under study is responsible.

Figure 4.1 is an example of a process map. This example shows the tasks included in the outprocessing of base personnel, which begins when responsible personnel are notified that an outprocessing is required. Individual tasks are added sequentially in a series of rectangles, with arrows showing workflow through the process. In this example map, not all tasks are required in each instance of the process. The third and fourth tasks in the sequence are dependent on a decision point (whether the member is a property custodian), displayed in a diamond-shaped

---

[2] Typically, a function is responsible for 50 to 100 distinct processes.

[3] AFMAA and the MRSs now archive relevant study data, which should eventually make this resource more valuable for future studies.

box. Contingent on that decision point, tasks two and three may be conducted, or the process may jump to task four.

Figure 4.1. An Example of a Process Map and Accompanying Detail

Process: 1.3. Out-processes Base Personnel
Input: Out-processing Required
Output: Out-processing Completed
Source of Count: Virtual Military Personnel Flight (vMPF) and Civilian Personnel Office (CPO)
Governing Directive: AFMAN 17-1203, Para 1.2.11.2.4.
Process Time: 11.11 minutes

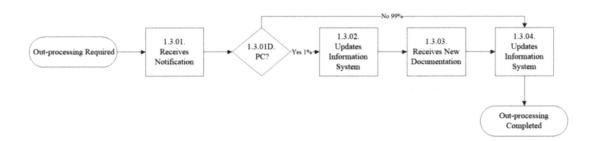

Table 3. Process 1.3. Out-processes Base Personnel.

Step	Activity	Activity Description	SAT
	Out-processing Required		
1.3.01.	Receives Notification	Logs into vMPF; logs into AIM; reviews appropriate fields; contacts CPO; logs out of AIM; and logs out of vMPF.	5
1.3.01D.	PC?	If member is a PC, go to 1.3.02; if member is not a PC, go to 1.3.04. **NOTE:** The decision is made and time is consumed in the previous activity. The decision activity just directs entity traffic to the correct route (not a measurable task).	
1.3.02.	Updates Information System	Logs into vMPF; logs into AIM; updates vMPF; updates AIM; freezes account; updates local tracker; logs out of vMPF; and logs out of AIM.	7
1.3.03.	Receives New Documentation	Receives appointment letter; receives loss or gain inventory; and receives Report of Survey (ROS) number.	4
1.3.04.	Updates Information System	Logs into vMPF; out-processes member; logs out of vMPF; logs into AIM; out-processes member; updates AIM; and logs out of AIM.	6
	Out-processing Completed		

SOURCE: Air Force Manpower Analysis Agency, 2017.
NOTE: PC = property custodian; SAT = standard activity time; vMPF = virtual military personnel flight; CPO = civilian personnel office.

Processes often include such decision-point-dependent tasks. The sequence of tasks is bounded at either end with markers for the process being triggered and completed. The process map is accompanied by macro-level information and a table with a short description of each task activity identified in the map. The average time to process each task, i.e., the standard activity time, and the overall average process time are also displayed, as well as the percentage of time the decision point is answered yes and no. We discuss these times and decision point weights in more detail later in this chapter.

In addition to drafting process maps, this information-gathering stage gives the study lead the opportunity to establish how to count the frequency at which each process is executed at each location (identified in the example in Figure 4.1 as "Source of Count"). An operational audit (AFMAN 38-102, 2019, pp. 95–103) is often used to determine required frequencies. Techniques include historical records, directed requirements, or technical estimates. *Historical records* may include electronic records or other historical reports, rosters, or other direct indicators. Indirect historical records, such as supply lists, may also be used, if applicable. A *directed requirement* is a predestined frequency for the process that has been established by a directive or policy. *Technical estimates* are established using the experience and judgement of experts knowledgeable of the process at each location. The basis for such estimates will vary. If a historical record is not available and if no directed requirement exists, a technical estimate of the process frequency must be used.

While the familiarization phase of a study results in a set of draft process maps and frequency resources for the function, it is the MRS study lead, not the functional experts, who documents and defines the workflow in practice. The lead spends considerable time on nonmanpower tasks to build a sufficient knowledge base to facilitate the actual manpower work. Knowledge will be lost if the lead is transferred to a new assignment prior to study completion. Transfers to new assignments happen much more frequently for active-duty airmen than for civilian manpower employees.

The Organizational Maturity Model

At the end of the familiarization phase, the MRS lead conducts a critical examination of the stability of the function using an organizational maturity model (OMM). The OMM informs function stability by iterating through a series of 20 questions across four domains: process, data, resources, and organization. *Process questions* inform policy and guidance, standard work, documentation, value streams, tracking initiatives, capturing lessons learned, and visual controls. *Data questions* review workload, performance metrics, requirements determinants, data systems, knowledge content management, and technology. *Resource questions* examine financial management, human capital allocation, assets, and facilities. Finally, *organization questions* inform effective communication, training management, and process improvement deployment strategy. Each question is scored on a five-level ordinal scale with a scoring rubric individualized to each question; individual scores are aggregated into an overall weight, with each question receiving equal weight.

The OMM analysis has three possible outcomes. The optimal result is that the function is judged to have sufficient stability, and the study continues. If some issues are uncovered that may be addressed simultaneously with the ongoing study, the study may still continue. In either case, the study moves forward to the workshop phase. The final possibility is that the function is judged to be lacking in ways that make it imprudent to attempt to move the study forward before critical items have been addressed. In this case, the study is discontinued. A potential course of action in this case is that a management advisory study is conducted instead, with the original manpower study to be reconvened at a later date under a new study charter.

Subject-Matter Expert Workshop

The study workshop convenes a group of SMEs in the essential work of the function. The workshop is usually a two-week event held at a common location, typically that of the MRS conducting the study. The SMEs discuss and provide information about the function critical to conducting the study and producing a manpower standard. Functional leadership chooses the SMEs, who are typically of senior rank among those in the function, selected across MAJCOMs, and should represent locations with a variety of workload volumes. The number of workshop participants depends on the number of locations in which the function is present; 10 percent of locations should be sampled when the function is spread over at least 100 locations.[4] The MRS organizes the event, including the logistics for all the attendees. In addition to the SMEs, representatives from functional leadership and the hosting MRS also attend.

The specific goals of the workshop are to verify the accuracy of the process map, provide average times for each task of each process, provide the proportion of time that decision-point-dependent tasks are executed within a process, identify sources for the frequency at which a process is executed, and review the process maps for potential improvement. These goals are addressed in two workshop components. The "as-is" portion examines process times and frequencies under current practice. The "to-be" component reviews current practice for potential improvements and resulting change in process times. Each component is discussed in greater detail below.

The Study Workshop As-Is Component

An MRS representative, typically the study lead, guides the SMEs through a discussion of each individual process map. The SMEs first discuss the tasks present on each map, ensuring that the tasks accurately describe the necessary work to complete the process and any decision points that may describe cases where certain individual tasks are or are not necessary for a given instance of a process. The process maps are adjusted as indicated by the discussion. Once the SMEs have confirmed the accuracy of a process map, they next discuss and build a consensus on the time it takes to complete each task and how frequently the decision point optional tasks are completed.

The goal of the task time estimation is to build consensus on the average time to complete each task (AFMAN 38-102, 2019, p. 105).[5] Our discussions with MRS staff and observations of live workshops reveal several concerns about determining this average. There is no standard format for eliciting the task times. In the workshops, we observed that, contrary to guidance, the

---

[4] An earlier version of AFMAN 38-208, Vol. I, contained a table equating number of locations to minimum workshop size (AFMAN 38-208 Vol. I, 2007, p. 70).

[5] AFMAN 38-102, 2019, provides a method for determining per-accomplishment times for tasks; however, the manual instructions do not specify a qualifier for the term *average*, such as conditions for the training or experience of the person executing the task. The goal is to find the functionwide average.

SMEs are often not instructed to focus on the average time. Asking more generally for task times could instead lead to a focus on a "typical" time, a median or mode, or a time sufficient for most of the occasions the process is carried out. Such phrasings as "how long does this usually take," "how long did this take last week," or "how long did this generally take last year" could lead to measures other than the average (Jacobs, 1998, p. 50). The lack of consistent, precise phrasing leads to additional ambiguity; for example, does one consider travel time or just touch time? Does one consider time required by inexperienced personnel or just experienced personnel? Each of these concerns allows the introduction of measurement error into the time estimates.

The most basic component of measurement error present in workshop time estimation or in filling out surveys involves the abilities of humans to accurately produce estimates of the time they spent completing a task. Published literature on this topic points to the potential for systematic inaccuracy in estimation, as opposed to random fluctuation about true mean task times. Multiple studies have found that people generally underestimate how long it takes to complete a task, often by 10 to 25 percent or even more (Kahneman and Tversky, 1977; Roy and Christenfeld, 2007, p. 560; Kruger and Evans, 2004). In addition to this overall tendency toward bias, the composition of SMEs at the workshop also may affect accuracy; various personal characteristics and relative experience with a task have been found to systematically affect duration estimates, including in surprising ways.

An individual SME may not have recent experience with every component task of each of dozens of processes; people who have just completed a task tend to underestimate task durations less (and are thus more accurate) than people whose experience of the task is less recent (Roy and Christenfeld, 2007, p. 561). SMEs in more-senior positions may not have actually executed a particular task in some time, making it difficult to recall an average time with precision without input from their subordinates. People who are experts at a task tend to underestimate task durations to a greater extent than relative novices, even after taking into account efficiency gains because of their expertise (Roy and Christenfeld, 2007, p. 561). Moreover, individuals in positions of power whose decisions affect others (such as managers) have also been observed to underestimate task durations to a greater degree than individuals not in a position of power (Weick and Guinote, 2010, pp. 597–599). Age can be another factor; adults older than 50 years have been found to underestimate tasks more than younger individuals (Espinosa-Fernández et al., 2003). Errors can compound if SME group composition is such that these factors introduce systematic bias all in a single direction. A workshop with older, more-experienced participants in managerial positions would thus be expected to underestimate task durations more than would a workshop staffed by younger, subordinate workers who had more recent, but less overall, experience with the task.

Finally, facilitation techniques and workshop discussion dynamics, beginning with the process mapping exercise, can play a role in the average task time estimates produced. This includes the extent to which the facilitator and group choose to break apart a single task into smaller and smaller subtasks, each of which receives its own duration estimate. Shorter-duration tasks tend to be underestimated less than longer-duration tasks, with potentially significant effects. One study found that people overestimated the duration 1-minute-long tasks by an average of 6 percent and underestimated 16-minute-long tasks by an average of 36 percent (Roy and Christenfeld, 2008, pp. 203–204). In general, disaggregating a task into small subtasks decreases underestimation and thus increases accuracy (Kruger and Evans, 2004).

The ways in which facilitators guide the group to arrive at a single duration estimate, with or without extensive group discussion, can also shift the end result. For example, in unstructured discussions, in particular, a small number of dynamic personalities among the SMEs could sway the individual estimates of other SMEs away from their otherwise best estimates of individual task times. Several studies have found that simply eliciting individual estimates, then averaging them to create a final group estimate, leads to less accurate results than eliciting individual estimates and then engaging in a group discussion with the aim of settling on a single consensus number (Fine and Vajsbaher, 2013, pp. 743–744; Moløkken-Østvold and Jørgensen, 2004; Sniezek and Henry, 1990). In the workshops, however, individual estimates are rarely gathered before the group discussion. More-structured approaches, such as the Delphi technique of multiround elicitation—in which individuals provide estimates, discuss and review others' inputs, and then make revisions—can increase accuracy (Rowe and Wright, 1999).

By design, the SMEs represent only a small proportion of locations at which the function is present. Some variation in task time is expected across locations (Air Force Manual 38-208 Vol. I, 2007, p. 77); this motivates the use of a sample of locations, instead of just one. The SMEs in the workshop draw on their own recent location experience in estimating average task times. A different small sample of SMEs would not provide identical task averages and might reach different consensus averages. This, along with the potential for systemic measurement error evident in the time estimation literature, as discussed earlier, raises doubts about the ability of the existing workshop process, as practiced, to produce valid, reliable estimates of process times.

For processes that involve decision points that determine whether some tasks within the process are needed, the workshop SMEs also generate an estimate of the proportion of the times these decision-point tasks are executed. Many of the same concerns that plague time estimation surface here as well, including the accuracy with which SMEs can recall these proportions; the suitability of individual SMEs to provide these estimates, given their most recent duties; and the dynamics of the personalities present at the workshop. One additional concern is more pronounced in this case: the effects of frequency distributions across locations. While it may be reasonable to think of the time it takes to complete a task as consistent across locations (i.e., the distribution of time it takes to complete a task applies to all locations), location-specific conditions, such as available resources, infrastructure, and equipment, may affect the proportion of times that decision-point tasks are needed. For example, a civil engineering help desk call may be resolved during the initial call or may require a visit to the caller's site. Locations with older infrastructure may require a greater proportion of site visits than those with newer infrastructure. This increases the likelihood that an estimate produced by a very small number of SMEs of the proportion of time that the decision point tasks are needed may not be representative of the true proportion across all locations.

Along with time estimation, SME workshop participants are expected to bring to the workshop or otherwise provide resources to collect the frequency of execution of each process at their locations. Some available data exist on the frequencies of certain processes, but estimates will be required for other processes. Estimation may occur within the workshops. As with time estimates, this introduces an opportunity to introduce measurement error into as-is estimates.

A final potential source of error in both time and frequency estimation, in a workshop or any other method for collecting SME inputs, involves the intrinsic motivation to overestimate time or frequency, given the known uses of the data. Underestimating these metrics could lead to insufficient manpower, adding to the burden on those executing the function, so there is motivation (intentional or unintentional) to overestimate. We did not discover any indications that such overestimation is occurring; however, the potential for such measurement error exists. A referee who has become sufficiently familiar with the function may be able to moderate instances of overestimation.

The Study Workshop To-Be Component

The U.S. Department of Defense (DoD) has asserted the value of continuous process improvement (CPI) for the sake of productivity, performance against mission, safety, flexibility, and energy efficiency and has directed the military departments to institutionalize CPI programs (DoD Directive 5010.42, 2008). The Air Force has directed AFMAA to conduct CPI events that inform standard work documents (AFI 38-401, p. 5). To address this requirement, the study workshop includes a process review component.

After validating the current process maps in the as-is step, the SMEs revisit each map to discuss opportunities for process improvement.[6] This process review is conducted at the level of detail present in the process maps. Potential improvements are elicited from the SMEs regarding the sequence of tasks necessary to complete a process. For processes with regular frequencies, the SMEs may consider what the *required* frequency should be, asking, for example, whether a monthly report could be done quarterly instead. Each suggestion is discussed, and the SMEs come to consensus on whether to approve each improvement idea. For each approved idea affecting the sequence of tasks, the SMEs discuss and provide updated time estimates for each task.

If the functional managers have the authority to do so, improvement ideas approved in the workshop may be directly implemented. The remaining ideas are tasked for later potential implementation and are taken up with the appropriate authoritative body. Time and frequency

---

[6] Our workshop observations revealed that there no uniform standard for when in the workshop to review for process improvement. The "as-is" component may be completed first and then all maps reviewed for improvement, or the process review could occur closer to the process map validation.

estimates for improvements approved and directly implemented are used in the study's development of required man-hours; estimates for the remaining improvements are saved for potential future updates, should the appropriate coordination and approvals be obtained.

In contrast to the desire for continuous or regular process improvement efforts, the workshop environment is episodic, occurring once every several years. While discussion of potential improvements to project tasks during the workshop seems pragmatic, given that each task of each process is directly examined in preparation for determining the required manpower, the rarity of the workshop is incompatible with the intended *continuity* of improvement efforts. Additionally, the small number of workshop participants is exclusive of the universe of sources of potential improvement ideas.

Aside from the characteristics of the workshop, the process maps are created at a level of detail that is valid for their intended purpose, describing the steps necessary to complete a process. While that level of detail may be suitably granular to consider individual task times to complete the process, the process map task descriptions do not provide the level of detail that would be necessary for in-depth process analysis and reengineering. Each task contains a series of mental and physical elements that are aggregated to produce the task. Any of these individual elements could be a source of waste or a barrier to workflow. Identification of potential measures to increase workflow, ergonomic efficiency, and safety and provide other gains requires examining each of these component elements (Damelio, 2011; Lehto and Landry, 2012). Our workshop observations reveal that, instead, the workshop process reviews are occurring at a broader level, considering each task as a whole but not thoroughly examining its components, which are not present in the process maps or accompanying task descriptions.

Development of Required Man-Hours

The metrics gathered at the workshop aggregate into a single value for each location: man-hours. Appendix B describes how man-hours are calculated in detail, but we discuss it briefly here. For an individual process, adding the average component task times provides an estimate of the average time to complete a process. In calculating this process-time estimate, times for tasks that follow decision points and are not executed every time are weighted by the proportion of time they occur. For example, a task that takes 10 minutes to complete but is only executed 20 percent of the time a process is performed would count as 2 minutes (10 minutes × 0.20) toward the average process time. While average process times are intended to apply to all locations, process frequencies are specific to each location at which the function is present. The individual (monthly) location frequency for each process is multiplied by the estimated average process time to calculate the man-hours needed for each process. These process-specific man-hours may then be added over all processes to produce an estimate of recent required man-hours at that location for the function.

Regression Approach to Required Man-Hours

The estimated recently required man-hours are a composite of the process times and frequencies for the dozens of processes for which the function is responsible. A conventional approach is to express this dense set of inputs by describing recent man-hour needs more succinctly, as a simple function of one or more workload factors (often referred to as *drivers*), most commonly through a regression equation. The workload factors are logical descriptors of the work performed by the function at each location; ideally, they are predictable and programmable measures. Examples of workload factors include the base population for functions that serve the needs of those present on the base and counts of equipment critical to function processes, such as the number of terminals for satellite communications. During the familiarization step described earlier, the MRS study lead has the opportunity to identify candidate workload factors.

The regression equation describing man-hours as a function of the workload factors then becomes the basis for the manpower standard. It generally takes a form similar to the following:

$$\tilde{y}_i = \alpha + x_i \beta + \varepsilon_i, \tag{4.1}$$

where $\tilde{y}_i$ is the estimated recently required man-hours per month at location i resulting from the workshop; x_i is a vector of current or projected workload factors; β is vector of workload factor coefficients; α is an intercept term; and ε_i is a normally distributed error term capturing the portion of man-hours that the drivers do not describe.[7] Using the available data, candidate regression models using different possible instruments are fit and examined. Because the process frequency information is collected only from the workshop participants in this approach, only a few data points are available for the regression exercise, typically 10 to 15 for functions that operate at a high percentage of locations and fewer for functions constrained to more-specialized locations. Because of this constraint, the number of drivers used in a regression must be small.

Finding the best model for describing man-hour needs using the workload factors requires examining a series of candidate regression models, each using one or more of the workload factors. Quadratic forms of individual workload factors (i.e., the workload factor value squared) may also be considered. Two metrics are used primarily to sort between the candidate regression models: the coefficient of determination (R^2) and the coefficient of variation (CV). R^2 describes the proportion of variation in man-hours described by the workload factors present in the model. The CV is a measure of how spread out the man-hour values derived from the workshop, $\tilde{y}_i$, are from their corresponding predicted values from the fitted regression line (i.e., it is a measure of the spread of the regression residuals).[8] R^2 values range from zero to one. CV takes nonnegative

---

[7] Alternative regression-based model forms are available, such as transforming the man-hours and workload factors in Equation 4.1 to a log scale (AFMAN 38-208 Vol. II, 2003, p. 74).

[8] The CV is calculated as the root mean square error of the residuals from the regression equation divided by the mean of the man-hour values used to fit the model.

values, and a CV < 0.25 is desired in finding a regression line to use as a standard. The minimum R^2 for considering a single driver in a model is set at 0.50; in practice, the regression models meeting the CV < 0.25 criterion and selected for a standard tend to have an R^2 in the range of 0.75 to 0.90.

Of the candidate regression models for the standard, the one with the highest R^2 and lowest CV is generally chosen, with deference to simpler equations when these statistics are similar across more than one model. Logistical checks are also performed on the potentially best model from these metrics, for example, checking that the required man-hours always increase with increasing values of the workload factor. The final chosen model is expressed as a standard, such as

$$y_i = a + x_i b, \tag{4.2}$$

where

y_i is the predicted man-hours from the fitted regression equation
a is the estimated value of the regression intercept α from Equation 4.1
b is a vector of one or more estimated regression coefficients β from Equation 4.1
x_i is the vector of current or projected workload factors.

For a given location, plugging the workload factor values, x_i, into Equation 4.2 provides the man-hours, y_i, for that location provided under the standard. The sum-product of b and x_i is the variable cost of manpower at each location, while a is the fixed cost common to all locations.

At times, the threshold values for R^2 and CV may not be met. In this case, multiple models for the standard may be used, each to describe the man-hour needs for a subset of processes. Similarly, if the manpower need is fixed for certain processes, the standard for these processes may be expressed as a constant, $y_i = a$. When such a modular approach is used, the required manpower across each component model is summed to produce the total man-hours required. Application rules are in place that address outlier locations, i.e., those with individual circumstances that make the standard derived from the regression deviate extensively from local needs and for which a variance is warranted. Additional rules address locations where the workload factor values require extrapolation to apply the standard, i.e., the workload factor values are too far above or below those present when the standard was developed (AFMAN 38-102, 2019, pp. 263–265).

The model comparisons and logistical checks performed on the model are essential to ensuring that the chosen model is not only the best fit but also pragmatic when serving as a standard. Linear regression models, however, come with a set of assumptions about the data being fit, and these assumptions are not always checked. For example, the distribution of the error term, ε_i, in Equation 4.1 is assumed to be the same across all potential values of the workload factors, as opposed to changing for different values of the drivers. Similarly, the fit of the model should be checked for excessive influence of an individual location on the equation the model produces. The procedures attributed to this process (AFMAN 38-102, 2019, pp. 211–268) do not address these standard regression steps.

Several additional concerns are present in the process typically used for gathering data for regression-based standards. As discussed above, the process for estimating man-hour observations used in the regression models contains multiple sources of measurement error, particularly in the development of average process times and, often, in collection of location process frequencies. Finding R^2 values in the range of 0.75 to 0.90 implies a strong model fit in terms of the overall relationship between the workload factors and man-hours; however, even these high values imply that the workload factors do not capture 10 to 25 percent of the variation in man-hours among locations, leaving the opportunity for the standard to misspecify the required man-hours. Because the workshop is attended by representatives of only a small number of locations, the standard is typically developed on 10 to 15 data points. This creates two additional concerns. The true R^2 over all locations may be misinformed using a sample this small and may not be as strong as the luck of the draw of a small sample may imply.[9] More important, selecting a different set of SMEs from different locations would produce a different standard; this would be true even if the measurement error in the man-hour calculations were not present but could also be exacerbated by the measurement error. Cumulatively, these concerns raise doubts about the precision of the standard produced.

To further explore the potential lack of precision in the regression-based standards, we constructed a simulation of the information that the workshop-based study process produces. In the following example, we simulate the development of a man-hour standard for a function present at 75 locations, with ten SME workshop attendees, and with the presence of a workload factor that has a true R^2 of 0.85 with the required man-hours. Appendix B discusses the details of the simulation exercise. The goal of this simulation exercise is to better highlight issues with inaccuracy that may occur using the regression-based approach to establish the standard; while the simulated function is hypothetical, the concerns illustrated are embedded into such applications. Figure 4.2 shows the simulated workshop-estimated man-hours for the locations of the ten SMEs (y-axis) and the workload factor (x-axis), along with the best-fitting regression line across the ten points. The regression model representing the simulated standard in Figure 4.2 presented an estimated R^2 of approximately 0.85 and a CV of 0.11, indicating acceptable values under the current process. However, the observation in the bottom left corner of the plot is highly influential relative to the other points on the plot—moving that point along the x- or y-axis would pull the line along with it.[10]

---

[9] Our focus here is not on the workshop methodology itself, but rather on the small sample size necessitated by workshop logistics. Our findings in this section would be true of any methodology that depended on a small sample size.

[10] A commonly used measure to investigate influence of individual points on regression results is Cook's D. Values of Cook's D greater than 1 are considered overly influential; the point in this example has a value of 1.65. This measure and others like it are not regularly employed in the model development.

Figure 4.2. A Simulated Example of a Regression-Based Man-Hour Standard

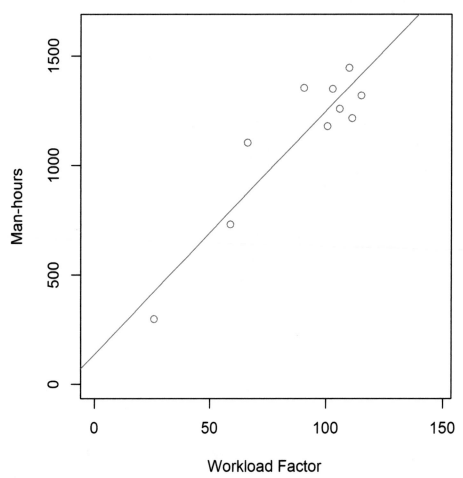

NOTE: The points in the figure represent simulated observations from ten SME locations. The line indicates the linear regression model fit to these observations.

Figure 4.3 contains data points from the remaining 65 locations for this simulated function, along with the original ten SME locations. These points represent the man-hours for these 75 locations based on the average process times generated in the workshop and their local driver values. Figure 4.3 also shows the best fitting regression line for all 75 points (the black line) along with the workshop-based regression line, originally seen in Figure 4.2, that would be used for the standard (the red line). As seen in the figure, although the regression line was a good fit for the original ten workshop data points, it appears high relative to the full set of 75 locations. Even though this particular simulated workshop found an R^2 extremely close to the true value, the regression line from the workshop locations does not translate accurately to the full set of locations.

Figure 4.3. A Simulated Example of Misspecification in the Man-Hour Standard

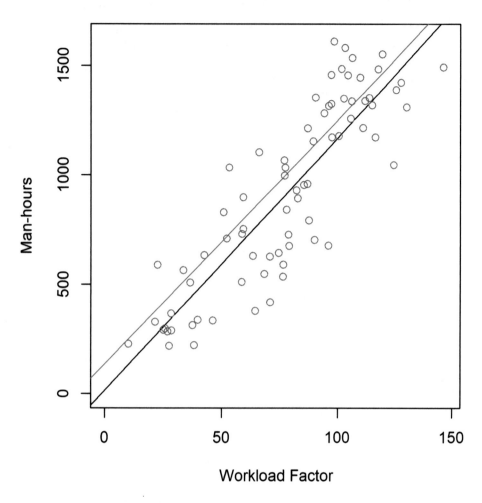

NOTE: The points in the figure represent observations from 75 simulated locations. The black line indicates the linear regression model fit to all 75 observations; the red line indicates the linear regression model fit to the subset of ten SME locations (identical to the red line in Figure 4.2).

As noted earlier, a choice of different SMEs could produce a different standard. Figure 4.4 illustrates this concern; it shows the original regression line along with the additional lines that would have been generated as the standard had benefitted from having different sets of ten SMEs from different locations participating in the workshop.[11] Considerable differences among the lines are present; for each unit increase in the value of the driver, the increase in required man-hours could vary by as much as 33 percent across the four potential standards in this example. In addition, one of the lines would have called into question the model using this workload factor as a potential standard because its CV is greater than 0.25. This simulated example helps illustrate

---

[11] To keep the plotting from becoming too dense, we simplified the example by using the same workshop-derived average process times as the original workshop. Thus, one may view the displayed differences among the lines as examples of how far the standard might deviate if the workshop had produced perfect average process times, i.e., a best-case scenario gives the measurement error present in the workshop time estimation.

the limitations on the potential for precision in the standard when using the SME workshop as the basis for the regression inputs.

Figure 4.4. A Simulated Example of Variation in Man-Hour Standard by SME Choice

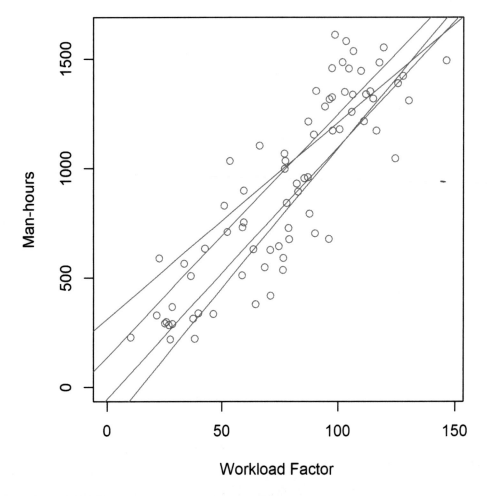

NOTE: The points in the figure represent observations from 75 simulated locations. The four red lines indicate the linear regression model fit to four distinct subsets of ten SME locations each.

To further explore potential imprecision in the standard generated through the workshop method, we replicated this simulation exercise 10,000 times, monitoring the predicted error rates in the regression-based standard,[12] and assuming no error in the workshop time or frequency estimates. The simulation parameters match the individual simulation discussed above, including a true R^2 of 0.85. Across all 10,000 simulations, the man-hour error rate typically ranged from

---

[12] The predicted error rate at a location is determining the positive difference between the actual required manpower and that predicted by the regression line (for example, the vertical distance from the regression line to an observation point in Figure 4.2), then dividing that difference by the actual required manpower.

9 to 36 percent,[13] with a median error of 19 percent; more than one-half of all predictions were off by at least 19 percent. At this median error, for every five FTEs of manpower predicted through the regression-based standard, the true need is likely to be approximately four or six FTEs. When we included a 10-percent underestimation of process times, as minimally suggested in the literature, along with 10-percent measurement error in the frequency counts, error rates increased to, typically, between 14 and 38 percent, with a median error rate of 25 percent. While the error rates correspond to a hypothetical simulated function and while error rates experience by real functions would differ, this example illustrates how significant prediction error at individual locations may be present, even when the R^2 indicates a strong fit.

Alternative Approach to Required Man-Hours

Regression-based approaches to establishing the required man-hours for a function at a given location are not always productive. For example, the R^2 and CV thresholds for model fit might not be met. An alternative approach, the *ratio unit times* or *ratio* approach, uses a ratio of man-hours to workload factor counts across all locations to establish the required man-hours for each location. Similar to the regression approach, the ratio approach linearly equates workload with man-hours; however, the ratio approach does not formally consider the equation error (the remaining portion of man-hours not described by the workload factor), instead establishing nonparametric estimates of the linear coefficients. In particular, this approach considers

$$\tilde{y}_i = \alpha + x_i \beta, \qquad (4.3)$$

which is identical to Equation 4.1, exception without the error term. Similar to the regression approach, $\tilde{y}_i$ is the estimated man-hours at location i resulting from the average time estimates from the workshop; x_i is a vector of one or more workload factors; and α and β represent fixed and variable man-hour coefficient components, respectively.

The procedure starts by mapping each process the function executes to a primary workload factor or factors that are expected to describe the man-hour need for that process (AFMAN 38-102, 2019). The expectation that the factor is a good descriptor may be based on logical considerations, which may be straightforward or observed in the familiarization phase. For example, the number of antennas present at a location may be a logical descriptor of procedures that cover antenna maintenance. Procedures that are mapped to the same workload factor(s) are grouped together, and a version of Equation 4.3 is considered for each group. The man-hour estimates across groups may be summed to produce the full man-hour requirement. Within each group, Equation 4.3 is estimated as follows:

- For each location, the total man-hours for procedures in the group are separated into fixed and variable needs. The classification of time as fixed may be rooted in particular characteristics of the procedures that are common to all locations at equal time cost, and a

---

[13] The typical range of the error rate noted is the range between the 25th and 75th percentiles of the error rate.

49

fixed component may not always be present. If more than one workload factor is being considered, the variable portion of the man-hours is further apportioned to each factor.

- For each workload factor, the variable man-hours mapped to that factor are totaled across all locations, and the count of workload factor units is also summed across all locations. The ratio of total man-hours divided by total workload factor units is then used as the estimate of the coefficient β for that workload factor, i.e., for a given workload factor, d, and group of procedures, g, the estimate, b_d, for the coefficient β_d is calculated as

$$b_d = \frac{\sum_{i=1}^{L} \tilde{y}_{ig}}{\sum_{i=1}^{L} x_i}.$$ (4.4)

Here, $\tilde{y}_{ig}$ is the estimated variable man-hours at location i for only the procedures in group g, and L is the total number of locations being used in the estimation.

- If a fixed component is present, the average fixed man-hours over all locations is used as an estimate, a, for the intercept α (see Equation 4.3).

Use of the ratio method is recommended when workload counts "do not vary widely from one location to another" (AFMAN 38-102, 2019, p. 275). It is more flexible to use than the regression approach in two significant ways. When the required man-hours are to be updated (for instance, if an improvement identified in the workshop to-be component is implemented), the updated time estimates may be plugged in for a simple revision of the affected ratio, and the new version of the standard is easily put in place. Conversely, the regression approach requires refitting and reevaluating the full regression equation. Second, if a procedure or procedure grouping is not present at a given location, it may be left out of the application of the standard.

While the ratio method may present some advantages, its ultimate purpose is still to find the best linear equation to describe the observed man-hour and driver data. Formal regression techniques are designed to optimize the fit of that equation, and the accuracy of this alternative ratio method is inferior.[14] Thus, investing in this method when the regression model did not produce a strong enough fit to meet minimum thresholds would yield even weaker options. In addition, the ratio method requires the user to make certain judgement decisions, including parsing fixed and variable man-hour contributions and mapping procedures to drivers, while the regression method would allow the data to describe these features. If a true fixed cost does exist and can be accurately identified, that cost could be accommodated through an alternative structure within the standard to compliment the regression results or could be subsumed into the regression, with the logical check that the fitted intercept is at least as large as the expected fixed component. Finally, we note that it may be shown that, when the variance in workload factor counts tends toward zero (i.e., when workload factor counts across locations tend to be the same), the ratio estimate of the linear coefficient β will approach the regression solution for a

---

[14] Technically, the method of least squares used to fit the linear regression models minimizes squared error loss, which is the sum of the squared differences between the observed man-hours and the man-hours predicted from the estimated equation. While the use of squared error loss is standard, other metrics could be considered. However, because the ratio method is not optimized relative to any specific loss function, better methods may be available for any loss function chosen.

model forced through the origin. Because the fixed man-hour need α is estimated in the minimization of model error, instead of assumed as an input for model fit, even in the best-case scenario of homogeneity in workload factor count across locations, the regression approach will improve the fit. Given the prediction error issues documented earlier for the regression method, opting for a method that allows even greater prediction error appears ill-advised. Alternatively, nonlinear model forms describing the relationship between workload factors and man-hours could be explored to improve model fit.

Additional Considerations

Coordination of Draft Standards

Once the MRS prepares a draft report documenting a standardized structure and required man-hours for the function, the report is vetted through a quality assurance process within AFMAA. Next, it is sent to the MAJCOMs for review and then, finally, to the functional manager. Lack of timely response in any of these steps may cause an unplanned delay in study completion. In addition, an objection from the functional manager at this stage could delay implementation.

Over calendar years 2016 and 2017, approximately 30 Air Force Manpower Standards were posted annually. Our discussions with the MRSs and AFMAA indicate that eliminating undue delays could increase the throughput, although the true potential gains are unknown.

Application of Standards After Development

After a standard has been fully coordinated with the affected functional manager and approved by AFMAA and AF/A1M, it is made available to the MAJCOMs with instructions regarding its implementation. At this point, MAJCOM manpower offices assemble workload factors for each of their locations, apply the standard, and update MPES. Since this process does not immediately affect allocation of funded manpower to the MAJCOMs, application of the standard would typically change only the number of unfunded authorizations in the function at each location.[15] However, the application does provide an occasion for MAJCOMs to reallocate existing funding across wings and activities for the activity that is under the standard.

In theory, MAJCOMs would reapply a standard whenever mission changes affected workload factors. In practice, MAJCOM and Air Staff manpower managers have advised us that reapplication seldom occurs.[16] Since reapplication would likely affect only unfunded authorizations, manpower managers see little benefit from it. We have also heard from Air Staff

---

[15] Exceptions would be if a standard reduced requirements by more than the number of unfunded authorizations or if the MAJCOM chose to redistribute its funded authorizations.

[16] AFI38-201 does call for a reapplication of manpower standards every two years or earlier if dictated by significant workload or mission changes.

and MAJCOM manpower managers and officials with Air Staff and MAJCOM programming experience that unfunded authorizations are seldom considered in manpower programming decisions. If so, reluctance to spend resources on reapplication of standards seems rational. However, if the relative proportion of unfunded authorizations in a function were used as a risk signal in Air Force programming and budgeting decisions, more-frequent reapplication of standards might play an important role.

To encourage more-frequent reapplication of standards, we recommend reducing the associated workload. Currently, an increase or decrease in unfunded requirements requires identification of specific authorizations to be added or deleted. In the case of added authorizations, a lengthy vector of position-level manpower characteristics must be developed and entered into MPES. This process could be streamlined by maintaining aggregate and/or abbreviated data on unfunded authorizations, i.e., total unfunded requirements at the level of category (officer, enlisted, or civilian) by organization, location, MAJCOM, functional account code, career specialty, and program element code. This would provide sufficient information for risk assessment in programming or funded manpower allocation decisions. MPES would have to be modified to accept the data in this form.

With better visibility of risk, commanders, programmers, and functional managers would be better equipped to make appropriate resourcing decisions. Potential actions to mitigate unacceptable risk would include changing work requirements in the standard work document, explicitly reducing levels of service, explicitly adopting a longer workweek, increasing funded authorizations, and directing other resources to the function (e.g., civilian employees, contractors, or reserve man-days).

5. Man-Hour Availability and Other Related Factors

For work that is covered under a manpower standard, the final phase of calculating a requirement is to convert the total amount of work into a number of positions that, if filled, will match the appropriate number of personnel to the workload. Converting required work into a number of positions necessitates information on how much work each person can supply in the relevant period (e.g., a month). As mentioned in Chapter 2, the Air Force uses several factors to make this conversion: a MAF that accounts for time when personnel are unavailable to work; an IAF that accounts for time spent on unmeasured, indirect work (i.e., overhead); an OLF that standardizes the acceptable level of overtime expected from personnel; and an allowance for personal needs, fatigue, and unavoidable delays (PF&D). Together, the methods behind these factors implicitly form the Air Force's policy for the appropriate level of personnel resources to allot for a given level of work.

In this chapter, we first summarize the methods for calculating each factor, then turn to potential sources of error and the theoretical impact each would have on the use of personnel resources. Finally, we discuss drivers of nonavailability that current factors do not account for.

Methods for Estimating Factors

The Air Force Manpower community uses a variety of methods to arrive at each of the four factors involved in calculating a requirement. This section summarizes the origin and methods that determine each factor.

Man-Hour Availability Factor

Methods in Recent Air Force Reports

After determining the volume of work that a given work center is expected to perform, the most important ingredient in calculating the required number of personnel is the amount of time that each person is available to perform productive work, which is known as the *MAF*. The current Air Force approach to calculating this factor takes the amount of time in a month that a given individual could theoretically work under different assumptions about the typical workweek (known as *assigned hours*) and subtracts estimates of the average amount of time that existing personnel are unavailable for legitimate yet nonproductive reasons (known as *nonavailable hours*).

As an example, one of the categories that renders an individual unavailable for work is leave.[1] To calculate the average amount of time an individual is assumed to be on leave, recent MAF studies request data on the total annual number of days personnel spent on leave in a three-year period and divide by the respective annual end-strength numbers to form a three-year average of the number of leave days per person per year. These studies then apply calendar adjustments to convert this into a monthly number measured in hours.[2] The MAF is formed by subtracting the nonavailable hours due to leave, along with monthly nonavailable hours from other recognized sources, from the assigned hours.

Methods for estimating the average nonavailable time for a given reason are similar to work measurement methods and tend to be data driven (Table 5.1). Average nonavailable time is measured either directly (for instance, by counting days of absence) or indirectly (through an output that drives the nonavailability). In the indirect case, the calculations multiply the output by the estimated average nonavailable time per instance and divide by the end strength to form an average time per person. Permanent change of station (PCS) moves illustrate this process well. During a PCS, a member must spend time out-processing at the departure point, shipping goods, settling into a new location, and in-processing at the destination. Administrative records do not capture the time spent on these activities, so the MAF calculations instead count the outputs (PCS moves, goods and car shipments) and multiply them by per-accomplishment durations reported in recent surveys to form an estimate of the average amount of time personnel are unavailable for work because of PCS activities.

Comparison of Air Force Man-Hour Availability Factors with Those of Other Services

Each branch of the armed forces must solve this problem of converting a certain amount of measured work into a number of positions, based on the amount of time a full-time person might be expected to work. Published guidance and documentation indicate that other services have adopted approaches similar to that of the Air Force, and (with the exception of the Coast Guard) arrive at similar results (Table 5.2). Further, the Air Force MAF is among the most up to date, having been renewed with recent data in 2016 (with a prior iteration in 2011).

---

[1] There is a debate centered around whether the MAF should count the full amount of *authorized* leave as nonavailable time, rather than the average amount of leave that members have taken. In practice, members take less than 2.5 days of leave per month, on average, for various reasons. New members might save leave to build up a balance; members can sell back unused leave; and members lose excess leave over a maximum balance at the beginning of a new fiscal year. Because the goal of the MAF is to accurately estimate the amount of time members are available to work, the use of empirical data on leave taken is appropriate. In the most recent MAF, a change in the calculation includes lost leave as a source of nonavailable time, which is inconsistent with this principle because lost leave does not reflect time that members are unavailable to work.

[2] The calendar adjustments also account for the fact that some leave does not affect availability because it is taken on weekends.

**Table 5.1. Sources of Nonavailable Time Included in the
2016 Military Peacetime Man-Hour Availability Factor**

Nonavailable Time Category	Activities Included	Outputs that Drive the Calculation	Inputs and Data Sources
Leave	Annual, emergency, convalescent, terminal, and lost leave	Measured directly	Total number of leave days taken and lost (finance data systems)
PCS	In- or out-processing, family settlement, shipment of household goods and cars	Total number of PCSs and total number of shipments	Average time per activity (survey data)
Medical	Inpatient, quarters, outpatient, ancillary, and dental visits	Measured directly	Total number of bed or quarters days, total number of visits, average time per visit by type (health data systems)
Organizational duties	Fitness testing, sponsoring new arrivals, individual personnel actions	Total number of fitness tests and total number of PCS moves; personnel actions are measured directly	Average time per fitness test, time required for sponsorship (SME interviews), average time spent on personnel actions (survey data)
Education and training	Promotion testing, some professional military education, ancillary training, and certain formal training	Total number of promotion tests and number of personnel attending professional military education; some education time is measured directly	Allotted promotion test time, number of academic days per course, time spent in formal training (personnel data)
Transition Assistance Program	Preseparation counseling, workshop, and other requirements	Total number of personnel separating or retiring	Allotted times for Transition Assistance Program activities

SOURCE: AFMAA, 2017.

**Table 5.2. Interservice Comparison of Monthly Nonavailable Hours and Availability
Factors, for Military Members on 40-Hour Workweeks During Peacetime**

	Air Force	Army	Navy	Coast Guard
Nonavailable category				
All training	4.2	—	6.4	4.9
Leave	8.9	—	11.4	10.1
Other reasons	5.3	—	4.3	20.5
Total nonavailable hours	18.5	22.3	22.1	35.5
Monthly availability	148.8	145.0	144.6	131.2
Year updated	2016	2006	2015	2012

SOURCES: AFMAA, 2017; AR 570-4, 2006; OPNAVINST 1000.16L, 2015.
NOTES: Navy and Coast Guard availability information is provided weekly, so the values in the table multiply the published values by the average number of weeks in a month. Army regulations do not list nonavailable time by category. Holidays are considered nonavailable time in other services but are not included in the table for consistency with the Air Force. If publications did not list a year that the availability factor information was updated, the year updated reflects the publication year.

Overload Factor

The OLF concept arose out of the principle that it is more efficient to accomplish some portions of a work center's mission through overtime than to staff the work center to the point of excess capacity. This principle gets implemented by specifying an acceptable level of overtime as a planning assumption in the process of converting measured workload into a number of positions. The OLF is thus the fractional amount of additional work employees are expected to bear before it becomes worthwhile to add another position. Both the Air Force and the Army adopt 7.7 percent as the acceptable overtime threshold; the Navy uses 7.2 percent for a standard, peacetime workweek.[3]

In publications of the other services, OLFs are called "fractional manpower cutoff points" or "breakpoints" because they originated as a way to cope with the fractional remainder when dividing man-hours by the availability factor. For instance, if a work center's manpower study called for 4.4 positions and if the calculation rounded down to four positions, the work of the additional 0.4 positions would be shared among the four personnel and would result in each person being overloaded by more than the acceptable overtime threshold. In a sufficiently large work center, any fraction of a position can be shared without exceeding the overtime threshold, so the Army and Navy guidance essentially implements overload factors as rounding rules for small work centers.

The Air Force implementation of this concept for military (but not civilian) requirements is to multiply the MAF by the OLF when applying a manpower standard and then to always round *up*. Like the other service methods, this adjustment also ensures that fractions of manpower never exceed 7.7 percent per person in a work center, but a key distinction in the Air Force method is that it continues to apply overload adjustments in ever larger work centers.[4] The result is that 7.7 percent becomes not just a cap on overtime in small organizations with fractional manpower requirements but an expectation of overtime in all predominantly military organizations.

To illustrate this concept, Table 5.3 shows the results of calculating the required number of personnel for varying military workloads and compares the Air Force approach of using the OLF with the Army's approach of resolving the fractional manpower using breakpoints. The first three rows show that, for small work centers, the Air Force and Army methods are identical and

---

[3] Internal reference documents AFMAA provided us show that the origin of the 7.7 percent figure can be traced back to an assumed limit of one-half hour per working day, using the MAF at the time that the rule was adopted in 1965, which was 142 hours per month. The Navy uses the same rationale for its figure; the *Navy Total Force Manpower Requirements Handbook* states that "A maximum individual work overload is established at one-half hour per working day" (Navy Manpower Analysis Center, 2000). Because the present day MAF has increased to 148.8 hours, an overload factor of 7.7 percent now equates to slightly more than one-half hour per workday.

[4] Per para 4.4.5.1, AFI 38-101, the OLF is applied in this way to military work centers and work centers with one to six civilian positions. Internal reference documents provided by AFMAA show that the application of the OLF to all work centers is the result of a change that took place in 1990. In earlier years, the OLF only applied to work centers with 13 or fewer authorizations and functioned similarly to the Army and Navy fractional breakpoint rules.

both avoid overburdening the work center with the fractional manpower. However, as the workloads increase, the Air Force method produces a smaller number of requirements because it continues to apply the OLF, while the Army method simply rounds the fractional manpower down.

Table 5.3. Comparison of Overload Factor Adjustment with Fractional Breakpoint Method for Varying Military Workloads

Man-Hours of Work	Personnel Required (work per MAF)	Rounded Requirement (OLF)	Rounded Requirement (fractional breakpoint)	Difference
100	0.67	1	1	0
500	3.36	4	4	0
1,000	6.72	7	7	0
5,000	33.60	32	33	1
10,000	67.21	63	67	4
100,000	672.09	625	672	47
200,000	1,344.18	1,249	1,344	95
500,000	3,360.44	3,121	3,360	239

NOTE: These calculations use the Air Force peacetime military MAF of 148.79.

In large work centers, the end result of this difference is that the Air Force calculation assumes personnel will work 2.7 hours of overtime per week *to accomplish their assigned tasks.* In a nontransparent way, it transforms the nominal 40-hour workweek into something longer than that. Natural fluctuations in workload and personnel availability could then necessitate further overtime in excess of the OLF to accomplish a work center's mission.

The actual impact of the OLF adjustment on requirements depends on the size of the typical work center in a functional area. The Air Force OLF adjustment would have very little effect on functions with only small work centers. Functions with large military work centers, however, would receive significantly fewer authorizations than the manpower requirement estimated under the fractional breakpoint method. To assess the effects of this, we used MPES data on total funded and unfunded requirements in each function within a unit (identified by personnel accounting symbol codes) to calculate the requirements each unit would receive under the fractional breakpoint method. For each case, we simulated rounding by subtracting a uniformly distributed random number between zero and one, multiplied the result by 1.077 to calculate the total FTE requirement, then applied the Army's fractional breakpoint rules to calculate the total requirement without the OLF adjustment. The result over 1,000 trials of simulated rounding showed an average of 4,195 authorizations, with a range of 4,137 to 4,246. That is, using the Air Force OLF adjustment resulted in 4,195 fewer total authorizations, which is work that the remaining personnel assigned to the relevant functions must accomplish. Further, more than

60 percent of this fell in just three functional areas: Security Forces (38 percent), logistics readiness (13 percent), and civil engineering (9 percent).

The Indirect Allowance Factor

Manpower determinants development processes focus on capturing direct work—that is, work involving activities that are "required by MAJCOM or higher directives, are essential to and directly support the work center's mission, and can be identified with a particular service or end product accurately, logically, and without undue effort or expense" (AFMAN 38-102, 2019, p. 88). In accomplishing a given workload, work centers also conduct activities that support the function but are not directly tied to an output or service. These tasks fall under the umbrella of indirect work and are captured through the IAF.

Because indirect work tasks are not specific to a particular function, AFMAA studies them separately in a cross-functional report. Still, the IAF study techniques strongly resemble the methods applied in studies measuring the productive work of a particular function. AFPC, 2015, identifies nine categories of indirect work and 105 measurable tasks within these categories. These categories cover personnel administration (civilian, officer, and enlisted), administrative support, meetings, training, supply, and work-area maintenance. After data collection and analysis, the report provides an estimated IAF by comparing the measured indirect work to the assigned manpower level. The IAF enters the calculation for the number of required positions by the measured workload (allocating a fixed proportional level of overhead) to form the total workload that is then divided by the MAF and OLF.

Personal, Fatigue, and Delay Allowance

The Air Force guidance mentions one additional type of factor, the PF&D allowance, under the procedures for work sampling. PF&D allowances are a flexible tool to capture different reasons that personnel might not be continuously contributing to productive work. Personnel require breaks to drink water or rest, and certain types of work might include inherent slack time for other reasons. PF&D allowances can be as simple as a fixed factor accounting for allotted restroom breaks or can include a customized factor based on a field measurement that applies only to an individual process under study (AFMAN 38-102, 2019, pp. 117–123). None of the reports that we reviewed mentioned the use of such factors, and Air Force manpower SMEs also indicated that they are not currently used. In theory, delays inherent in work processes would be captured and allocated time credit in the estimation process (see Chapter 4), but it does not appear that functions generally receive manpower credit for miscellaneous breaks during a duty day.

Evaluating Potential Sources of Error in Man-Hour Availability Factor Measurement

The Consequences of Man-Hour Availability Factor Errors on Staffing

Before discussing potential sources of error in MAF measurement, it is useful to first consider how MAF mismeasurement would affect staffing at the aggregate level. Here we consider two types of measurement errors that have different implications: (1) the MAF could systematically over- or underestimate availability, but the error could be consistent across functions, or (2) the MAF could over- or underestimate availability in a way that differs across functions. For simplicity, we focus on overestimation of availability in the following illustrations, but the principles are consistent in the reverse if the MAF were to underestimate availability.

When considering only the total requirement for a single function as determined by the application of manpower standards, an overestimation of the MAF will result in a requirement level that is lower than the level needed to perform all of the measured work. This is because an overestimation assumes the average person will contribute more hours of work than he or she actually can, which causes the requirement to fall below the true need. However, ACS functions are not typically staffed at the level of the total requirement, but rather, manpower standards are an input (or a signal) into decisions concerning where to place funded authorizations. The impact of overestimating the MAF, then, depends on how standards enter into funding decisions.

To illustrate the potential effects of MAF error, Figure 5.1 depicts a simplistic example in which a notional manpower planner is allocating funded authorizations across only two functions. In each case, the planner has a fixed number of funded authorizations to spread across the two functions according to one of two sets of funding rules. The first column shows cases in which the planner decides to fund the same percentage of the perceived requirement in each function (which differs from the true requirement because of MAF error). The second column shows cases in which the planner fully funds what he or she perceives to be the requirement in function "A" and allocates the remainder to function "B." The rows show results for different types of MAF error—either with the MAF overestimation being "systematic" (i.e., the same in both functions) or with the MAF overestimating availability in only one of the two functions. In each panel of the figure, the Desired bar indicates what the planner would do with a correctly estimated MAF, and the Actual bar indicates the result in which the MAF error occurs. The gap between the True Requirement and the height of the bars represents requirements that are invisible to the planner because of the MAF error.

Figure 5.1. Example of Planner Allocating Funded Authorizations Under Various Funding Rules and MAF Errors

First, to help guide interpretation, consider the case (represented in panel I) in which the MAF is systematically overestimated and the planner seeks to fund the same percentage of requirements in both functions. If there were no MAF error, the Desired bars indicate that the planner would place the same numbers of funded and unfunded requirements in each function. The result of the error in this case is that the planner fails to accurately represent the shortages with unfunded requirements but still arrives at the desired level of funding in both functions. Thus, if the pool of funded authorizations is being shared equally and if the MAF error is consistent across functions, the error does not result in misallocated resources.

But the cases in panels II through V indicate that MAF errors tend to result in too little funding in areas where availability is overestimated. In panel III, for instance, the planner still seeks to fund the same percentage of the requirement in both functions but ends up placing too few funded authorizations in function A and too many in function B. If the planner had a correct MAF for each function, he or she would have allocated more funded and unfunded authorizations to A rather than sharing them equally across the two functions. Thus, overestimating the MAF will tend to cause planners to underfund the affected functions because it obscures their view of the true requirements. This simplistic representation suggests that decisionmakers consider carefully whether a given MAF accurately represents availability in a function, especially if funding that particular function is a priority over others.

Potential Sources of Error

Turning to the real-world application of Air Force manpower standards, the MAF could theoretically fail in its purpose of representing the amount of time a member is available to work in three general ways:

1. The MAF could overestimate availability if significant sources of nonavailability were omitted from consideration.
2. The MAF could over- or underestimate availability because of data limitations or other reasons that precluded accurate estimation of nonavailable time.
3. The Air Force–wide average might poorly represent the realized availability for work in certain sectors.

We explored the first possibility in our review of recent MAF study reports and in discussions with personnel at AFMAA, the MRSs, and some interview participants from private industry. The most significant source of nonavailability that consistently arose in discussions with Air Force personnel was deployment participation. Although procedures were formerly in place for awarding manpower credit for deployments (AFMAN 38-208, Vol. I, 2007) and interview participants and prior studies indicated that deployments had previously factored into manpower standards, current practices contain no link between deployments and manpower authorizations. The next chapter explores this source of nonavailability and alternatives for capturing deployment demand in the manpower system.

Some additional sources of nonavailability time arose in discussions. The MAF accounts for ten holidays per year, but MAJCOM commanders often authorize additional days off in conjunction with key holidays (known as *family days*), which reduce availability but are not currently part of the MAF. Further, many common reasons for nonavailability are covered under the umbrella of permissive temporary duty (PTDY). PTDY is the vehicle for providing members time to secure off-base housing when relocating (up to ten days) and for preseparation or retirement relocation activities such as job or residence search (up to 20 days). PTDY is also used to implement the Military Parental Leave Program, which authorizes nonchargeable leave of up to 42 days for primary caregivers and up to 21 days for secondary caregivers following qualifying birth events or adoptions (Air Force Guidance Memorandum 2018-90-01, 2018). We discussed the inclusion of these categories of nonavailable time with specialists at AFMAA, who indicated that they are working toward incorporating PTDY-related nonavailability adjustments, subject to the availability of data in Air Force leave accounting systems.

Our review of MAF study reports and discussions with AFMAA specialists yielded no reason for concern about data limitations. Nearly all estimates of the average nonavailable time for the various reasons rely on official data requests and reasonable analytic methods. Although an audit of the data themselves was beyond the scope of this study, there is no reason to think such methods would not produce accurate estimates of the average times Air Force personnel are unavailable for productive work.

The third potential threat to MAF validity could occur if different sectors of the Air Force workforce systematically diverged from the Air Force–wide average in an aspect of work availability. Current policies differentiate MAF estimates by personnel category (military versus civilian) and contain specialized MAFs for firefighters, USAFA instructors, overseas personnel on extended workweeks, and foreign nationals for some overseas basing locations (AFI 38-101, 2019, p. 23). Though we could not explore this question empirically, discussions with AFMAA personnel indicated that, at the time of this writing, there was no demand signal from communities desiring further customization to the standard MAFs. AFMAA could consider whether systematic monitoring of function-specific deviations from the Air Force–wide MAF would be more effective than relying on functional area representatives to request customized MAF studies.

6. Deployment Credit

Contingency deployment of ACS personnel is used to provide base support functions at deployed locations. Deployments from garrison ACS functions to meet these needs differ from deployment of garrison warfighting units and their equipment in that ACS garrison workloads generally are not reduced as a result of the deployment.[1] Air Force policy provides that commanders should consider garrison support requirements when making manpower available for deployment, but that units should "defer or reduce performance standards to allow maximum deployment participation" (AFI 10-401, 2012, p. 182). This policy was probably conceived with intermittent demands in mind, but decades of continuous deployment demand have resulted in varying levels of workforce stress, degraded garrison service levels, or some combination of the two.

To mitigate these effects, a 2007 change in manpower policy provided for deployment credit in manpower determinants for ACS functions (AFMAN 38-208 Vol. I, 2007, pp. 107–110, since superseded; the superseding document, AFMAN 38-102, 2019, does not prescribe deployment credit). The credit was structured as a man-hour addition to other man-hour calculations in a manpower standard. However, because of fluctuating deployment demands at various locations associated with the air and space expeditionary force (AEF) deployment cycle, with most units vulnerable for deployment in one out of three periods, application of deployment credit provisions proved to be impractical and was not implemented. Nonetheless, ACS functional managers continually cite deployment credit as an unmet need.

This chapter outlines a method for providing deployment credit in unit manpower authorizations that, for sufficiently large manpower pools, can vary with approximately the same size and timing as deployment demands. The credit would depend in part on historic patterns of deployment demands and in part on fine-tuning by designated Air Force offices of responsibility, for example, at MAJCOMs, the Air Force Installation and Mission Support Center (AFIMSC), or AFPC, responsible for distributing and monitoring deployment taskings.

Changing Patterns of Deployment Demands

While a garrison unit's deployment demands still fluctuate over the course of the AEF cycle, we found that these fluctuations are not as wide as those that occurred when the deployment

---

[1] We use the term *garrison* in this discussion to refer to the home stations from which ACS personnel are deployed. Thus, *garrison ACS functions* are those whose purpose is to provide support services at home stations and whose manpower standards are based on garrison servicing requirements. These functions are identified in Table 3.10 in AFMAN 38-208 Vol. I, 2002. (The list was compiled in 2007, so should be reviewed and may require updating.) Garrison ACS functions do not include contingency units, such as Red Horse civil engineering squadrons and combat communications squadrons, that have no garrison support responsibilities.

credit provision was first established in 2007. The three charts in Figure 6.1 illustrate quarterly deployment fluctuations at the wing and function (defined by functional account codes) level during three periods bounded by key policy changes. The three examples in these charts track the proportion of a wing's garrison workforce deployed during a fiscal quarter for three function and major command combinations: civil engineering in Air Combat Command (ACC), security forces in Air Mobility Command (AMC), and services in Air Education and Training Command (AETC). In all three cases, fluctuations across fiscal quarters were wide during the years prior to 2009 but narrowed significantly that year, when the Air Force shifted to a policy of tasking wings for two periods out of three rather than one period out of three. In 2015, fluctuations again widened somewhat as the Air Force shifted to a policy of deploying larger groups from fewer units (intended as a resilience measure). Additionally, the civil engineering and security forces charts clearly show gradually diminishing deployment demands between 2008 and 2014.

While overall ACS deployment rates have diminished somewhat, many functions are still heavily tasked. In 2016, the last year for which we have comprehensive data on completed deployments, the most heavily tasked functions averaged more than 12 percent of their garrison strengths deployed at any time (see Figure 6.2). The overall average was more than 8 percent.

Dynamic Deployment Credit

Given this continuing level of deployment demand, we looked for an approach that would make it feasible for the Air Force to resource, rather than degrade, the levels of garrison service in ACS functions. The approach we identified can be termed *dynamic deployment credit*.[2] It would require that the Air Force fund a pool of manpower authorizations sized to about the average number of personnel expected to be deployed from ACS garrison support functions. The pool would be distributed to MAJCOMs according to their expected deployment taskings and would be further distributed within MAJCOMs to functional areas and units, also according to expected deployment taskings. MAJCOM manpower management offices would update MPES to show the distributed authorizations, identifying them with a new manpower standards implementation code specific to this purpose.

Deployment-credit authorizations would be much more dynamic than traditional authorizations. As with traditional authorizations, they would have a time dimension extending over future fiscal quarters but would routinely change from quarter to quarter as expected deployment demands changed. While historic trends can provide a reasonably good forecast of future deployment demands (as we will discuss in the next section), we visualize that MAJCOM functional area managers, who are responsible for management of deployment taskings, would also be responsible for distributing deployment-credit authorizations.

---

[2] Other approaches could be used to backfill the portions of the workforce absent from the garrison for deployment. In our discussions, manpower stakeholders mentioned increased overtime, additional contractor support, and reserve component augmentation.

Figure 6.1. Deployment Demands by Wing and Function

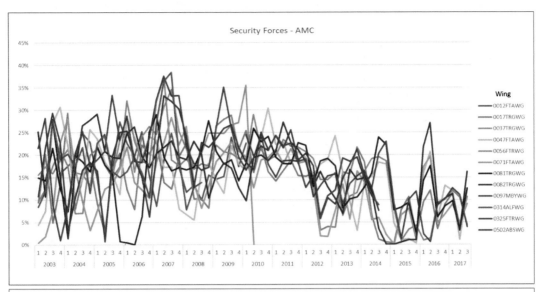

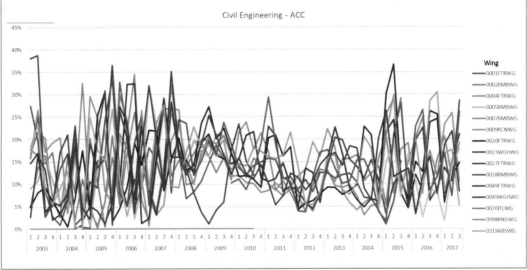

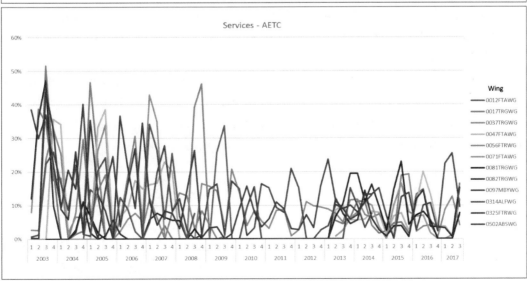

65

Figure 6.2. Proportion of Garrison Strength Deployed, by Function, FY 2016

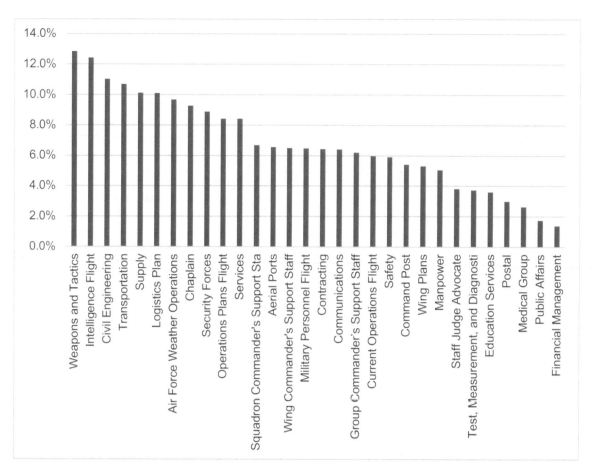

To avoid additional assignment turbulence, which is costly from both the individual and institutional perspectives, the process would depend on the turnover related to separations and rotational PCSs to keep garrison assigned strengths at or close to fluctuating requirements. Conveniently, enlisted assignments are determined in quarterly cycles, coinciding with the time periods used for projected manpower authorizations. To influence assignments, deployment credits in the fiscal quarter targeted in the next assignment cycle would have to be updated no later than the start of preparations for the assignment cycle. Because of this reliance on natural turnover for strength adjustments (which we will discuss more in the next section), the process would be used primarily for high-density requirement—those large enough to experience multiple gains and losses each quarter. This would probably exclude requirements for officers, senior noncommissioned officers (NCOs), and some smaller functions.

Natural Turnover

Units continually experience turnover because of the separation or reassignment of members. Losses are replaced by reassignments to the units in approximately the same numbers. Turnover rates are high enough to allow some range of strength adjustments simply by providing more gains than losses for increasing requirements or fewer gains than losses for decreasing requirements in an assignment cycle. The turnover rate does not limit how much a unit's strength can be increased in an assignment cycle because the large number of individuals available for assignment in a cycle relative to a specific unit's requirements would allow gains to exceed losses by indefinite amounts. However, assuming that no additional reassignments are generated to balance unit strengths, the turnover rate does limit how much strength can be reduced in an assignment cycle—with zero gains, a unit's strength will be reduced by the number of losses experienced during the cycle. Thus, the primary concern in using the assignment process to fill dynamic deployment credits is that a unit resourced to fill a large demand in one quarter may be overresourced in the following quarter if the quarter-to-quarter drop in demand is too great. To determine the likely prevalence of this problem, we examined turnover rates and their relationship to changing deployment demands within base-level functions.

Turnover rates can be calculated from observed tour lengths. For ACS enlisted personnel in CONUS units, we determined that the average tour length in recent years (FYs 2014 through 2016), including tours terminated by either reassignment or separation, is 3.5 years. The annual turnover rate is the reciprocal of the tour length—28.2 percent. The average turnover rate in a quarterly assignment cycle is one-fourth of that rate, or 7.1 percent. As Figure 6.3 indicates, enlisted turnover is seasonal, with more gains and losses during the spring and summer than in the fall and winter. Given the loss patterns shown here, we would expect quarterly turnover rates to be 6.5 percent, 6.9 percent, 8.7 percent, and 6.2 percent, respectively, for the first through fourth calendar quarters.

Comparing the average quarterly turnover rate to changes in quarterly deployment demand allowed us to estimate how often natural turnover could be depended on to keep unit strengths aligned with dynamic deployment credits. If a unit's strength were increased to meet deployment demands in a quarter, would expected attrition without replacement be sufficient in the next quarter to draw the unit's strength down to its normal level? We examined quarter-to-quarter changes in the proportion of CONUS ACS personnel deployed from bases and functions in two periods: 2011 to 2014, when fluctuations in base and function deployment taskings were minimized through the two-out-of-three-periods policy, and 2015 and 2016, when the larger-groupings-from-fewer-units policy was in effect. The results (Table 6.1) indicate that deployment requirements, as a proportion of total available strength, would drop by more than the 7.1 percent average quarterly turnover rate in only 10 to 15 percent of cases for base functions with larger (greater than ten) total requirements but would be more problematic in smaller functions.

Figure 6.3. Enlisted Strength Turnover in CONUS ACS Functions, Calendar Year 2014–2016 Averages

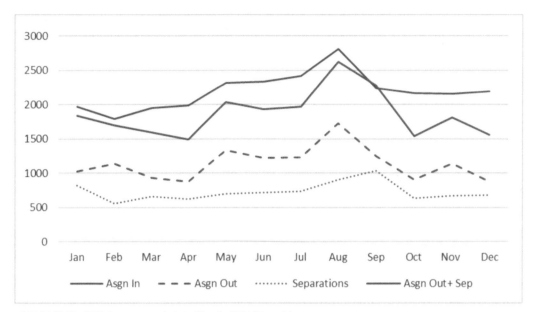

SOURCES: AFPC personnel data files in RAND archives.
NOTE: Gains exceed losses because strength grew in 2015 and 2016. Enlisted end strength was 250,104 in FY 2014 and 252,762 in FY 2016 (Defense Manpower Data Center, undated).

Table 6.1. Enlisted Quarter-to-Quarter Changes in Proportion of Base or Function Deployed

Period	Changes	Large[a]	Small	All
2011–2014	Total nonzero changes	7,279	3,128	10,407
	Total positive changes	3,378	1,499	4,877
	Total negative changes	3,901	1,629	5,530
	Changes < –7.1 percentage points	716	1,237	1,953
	% changes < –7.1 percentage points	9.8	39.5	18.8
2015–2016	Total non-zero changes	3,347	1,067	4,414
	Total positive changes	1,804	494	2,298
	Total negative changes	1,543	573	2,116
	Changes < –7.1 percentage points	505	427	932
	% changes < –7.1 percentage points	15.1	40.0	21.1

SOURCE: Data are from AFPC's AEF Operations and Readiness Division.
NOTES: Data are for CONUS MAJCOMs only. Nonzero changes are changes occurring when there are deployments in either or both of two contiguous quarters.
[a] Large Wing/FAC combinations are those with more than ten personnel assigned.

Forecasting Demand

Placing dynamic deployment credits in the right units and functions would depend on how accurately future deployment demands can be forecast. Our analysis of deployment data for the 2003 to 2016 period provides some encouraging findings. At a wing and function level, for larger functions (populations of 100 or more), the quarterly average number of deployed ACS personnel over any two-year period correlates well ($r^2 = 0.48$) with the demand three quarters later. As Figure 6.4 indicates, if this simple method were used to distribute deployment credits, credits would match deployment demand about one-fourth of the time. In another one-fourth of cases, credits would match demand within one. In 78 percent of cases, they would match within five. The knowledge of MAJCOM functional area managers, whose formal responsibilities include management of deployment taskings and sourcing, would significantly improve the matching of credits to demand over this simple method). In our proposed concept, the same MAJCOM functional area managers would be responsible for distributing dynamic deployment credits.

Figure 6.4. Accuracy of Deployment Forecasts Based on Recent History

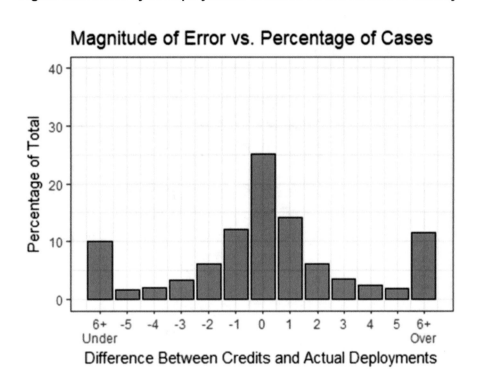

Sizing the Dynamic Deployment Credit Pool

As Figure 6.5 shows, deployment demand has declined during the past decade. The most recent two years for which we have complete data (FYs 2015 and 2016) indicate that enlisted ACS deployments involved around 5,000 individuals at any given time. That is approximately the size of the pool that would be required to fully offset deployment demands on garrison functions. A smaller size could be programmed if the proposed distribution process focused only on larger functions with more-consistent turnover rates (thereby minimizing potential overresourcing of some units) or if some continuing risk of degraded levels of service were to be accepted.

This approach would address steady-state deployment demands but would likely not be viable during a surge. A surge might not be foreseen with the lead time needed to program additional manpower resources. Tasking patterns during a surge would probably vary from the rotational patterns evident in steady-state taskings. On the other hand, a surge does not present the sustained, long-term erosion of service levels that this proposal is intended to offset.

Figure 6.5. ACS Deployment Demand

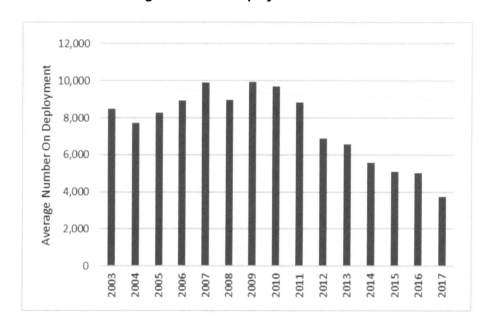

7. Feedback Loops

Systems theory visualizes an organization as a *system* that uses *processes* to transform *inputs* (resources, including manpower) into useful *outputs* intended to produce desired *outcomes*. Systems theory also posits the utility of *feedback loops* to determine how well a system is working. Feedback loops measure trends in various aspects of outputs and outcomes and provide a basis for adjusting either inputs or processes to improve system performance.

In this context, Air Force manpower determinants are used to estimate the manpower inputs needed to produce airpower and other related Air Force mission-related outputs. As indicated in earlier chapters of this document, these estimates are subject to error in their initial development or to obsolescence because of changes in work processes. With scarce resources available for manpower measurement, the Air Force must choose where to apply its capacity for updating manpower standards. Ideally, these choices would be guided by feedback loops.

Our experience with Air Force manpower processes suggests that such feedback loops tend to be subjective and unsystematic. When manpower shortages appear to affect mission accomplishment, commanders may convey their concerns to more-senior commanders in their chains of command, and these concerns can sometimes result in either leadership-directed reallocation of manpower at the MAJCOM or Air Staff level or to program changes implemented through the Air Force corporate structure. Similarly, MAJCOM or Air Staff functional managers may sense and convey shortages that can lead to manpower changes.[1] Notably, while these feedback loops may produce ad hoc changes in manpower inputs, they do not directly affect manpower standards and, therefore, do not improve the systematic determination of manpower requirements.

In this chapter, we explore several feedback loops that could be used to more objectively and systematically signal the need to update or adjust manpower determinants. We visualize two potentially useful indicators. One would be the time personnel in various functions spend on the job. Another would be the levels of service attainable within various functions.

Time on the Job

In staffing studies done for private-sector or civil-service workforces, the amounts and patterns of overtime usage can provide useful feedback regarding the adequacy of the workforce size. While some overtime usage may be economically favorable for both employers and employees, heavy and sustained (i.e., not seasonal or episodic) overtime usage provides a strong

---

[1] Some reprogramming actions can be triggered by the update or reapplication of a manpower determinant. However, we are referring here to reprogramming that occurs without such an update or reapplication.

indicator of an inadequate workforce size. In contrast, the absence of overtime usage, particularly when the level of service is perceived to be adequate, undercuts claims for additional manpower resources. For military personnel, there is no timekeeping system to provide this feedback. However, we believe that a reasonably good proxy for timesheet data could be constructed, at minimal cost, using a survey approach.

Our proposal is to place a time-on-the-job item in a recurring survey. While some research would be required to determine the best way to word the item, the following example likely contains the key elements:

> How many hours per week do you typically spend performing your current military duties? Include on-the-job rest and bathroom breaks but not lunch or individual fitness breaks. Base your estimate on weeks with no leave, holiday, or other absences from work.

Individual responses to this item would likely be biased, either intentionally or unintentionally. Research could be conducted to determine the direction and magnitude of biases, providing a basis for systematic correction of responses. However, even without correction for bias, reported means and variances would likely differ by function, location, grade, or other factors. Relative differences, particularly among functions or locations, would provide meaningful feedback that could inform both the construction of manpower determinants and priorities for updating them.

An item such as this would best fit in a survey that otherwise focuses on workforce measurement. Fortunately, the Air Force routinely employs such an instrument: the occupational analysis surveys used to determine job content. Functions are surveyed on a three- to four-year recurring cycle. The results are used to inform training course content, promotion testing subject matter, and other similar occupation-related needs. The surveys are constructed, administered, and analyzed by an occupational analysis division within the AETC Studies and Analysis Squadron. The squadron commander and responsible division chief have indicated a willingness to incorporate such an item in the surveys. Conveniently, this occupational analysis activity is located on Randolph Air Force Base in close proximity to AFMAA.

Performance Metrics

Performance metrics provide another indicator of the adequacy of system inputs. Performance of a system is affected by all resource inputs, not just by manpower resources, and is also affected by process design. Good performance metrics provide some assurance that all inputs are adequate. Poor metrics indicate a need to examine inputs and processes to determine root causes. For Air Force ACS functions, sets of performance metrics are available for this purpose, calibrated to the defined *levels of service* known as Common Output Level Standards (COLS). AFIMSC maintains the level-of-service definitions and associated performance metrics. COLS are intended to contribute to decisionmaking and risk analysis by guiding how resources (money and manpower) are programmed (AFIMSC, 2018). Like manpower standards, they are tied to program element codes and functional account codes. However, for reasons that remain unclear to us, a recent decision was made to disassociate COLS from manpower programming decisions.

COLS are measured at four levels of impact (see Table 7.1), with level 1 indicating full support and levels 2 through 4 indicating increasing risk. AFIMSC officials indicate that some functional managers have augmented these definitions with function-specific criteria for each level. COLS target levels are set prior to each programming cycle through an iterative process involving AFIMSC, functional managers, and the Air Force corporate structure. As Table 7.2 indicates, COLS for many ACS functions were set at levels other than 1 in FY 2018—a sign that risk is being deliberately managed in light of scarce resources.

Table 7.1. Common Output Level Standards

Level	Title	Definition
1	Full support	Provides fully effective and efficient mission capability and compliance with DoD, Air Force, and statutory legal requirements with negligible risk to mission, force, and/or institution. Resources (funding and manpower) are programed and/or available to reasonably ensure successful mission outcome(s) at an optimum level of service.
2	Minor impact	Accepts minor risk to mission, force, and/or institution but maintains an acceptable level of mission effectiveness and efficiency. Because some risk is taken at this level, not all DoD or Air Force regulatory requirements may be met, but all statutory legal requirements must be met. Resourcing levels are reduced commensurate with this reduced level of service.
3	Moderate impact	Accepts significant risk to mission, force, and/or institution. It allows for decreased mission effectiveness through reductions in noncore mission capabilities. It also allows for the failure of non–mission-critical support programs and activities. Compliance with only the most mission-critical DoD and Air Force and regulatory guidance is maintained. All statutory legal requirements must continue to be met. Resourcing levels are reduced commensurate with this reduced level of service.
4	Major impact	Provides only the minimum amount of support necessary to sustain core operational mission capabilities and statutory legal requirements and permits substantial risk to mission, force, and/or institution. Incurred risks have the potential to create substantial mission degradation or unrecoverable program failure if sustained for an extended period. As a result, Level 4 should be used only as a temporary, short-term measure. If this level is intended to be sustained over the long term, the Air Force corporate structure should consider divestment of the capability from the Air Force portfolio and associated resource reductions in the Air Force Planning and Programming processes.

SOURCE: AFIMSC, 2018.

Table 7.2. Air Force COLS—Fiscal Year 2018 Levels

Function	Level	Function	Level	Function	Level
BSV&E Management	2	Facility Sustainment	3	Materiel Management	1
BSV&E Operations	2	MFH Overseas	2	MILPERS	2
BSV&E Procurement	3	MFH Privatized	2	MWR—Fitness	2
Chaplain Corps	2	Financial Management	2	MWR—Libraries	3
Child and Youth Services	1	Fire Emergency Services	2	MWR—ODR	3
Civilian Personnel Services	3	Food Services	2	Pavement Clearance	2
Contracting Operations	4	Grounds Maintenance	3	Pest Management	3
Custodial Services	3	Inspector General	2	Petroleum & Cryogenics	1
Cyberspace Operations and Information	3	Installation Emergency Management	1	Protocol	2
Environmental Quality	3	Installation Movement	2	Public Affairs	3
Engineering Planning and Integration	3	Installation Safety	1	Security Services	4
Geobase	3	Laundry and Dry Cleaning	2	Unaccompanied Housing	4
Equal Opportunity	1	Legal Support	1	Warfighter & Family Readiness	3
Facility Demolition	4	Lodging	3		

SOURCE: AFIMSC, 2018.
NOTES: BSV&E = Base Support Vehicles and Equipment; MFH = Military Family Housing; MILPERS = Military Personnel; MWR = Morale, Welfare, and Recreation; ODR = Outdoor Recreation.

Figure 7.1 gives an example of COLS performance targets for one function (financial management). This example seems to provide good indicators of key performance outputs of the function. We reviewed a variety of performance targets for other ACS functions and found an uneven level of quality, including some that measured inputs, such as manning levels, rather than output performance. However, if refined and fully integrated into formulation of Air Force programs and budgets, COLS and their related performance targets have the potential to improve Air Force resourcing decisions.

Tandem Application

If used in tandem, time-on-the-job and performance metrics would provide stronger signals than either feedback loop used alone. High time on the job combined with low performance as measured by COL metrics would signal a very strong possibility of manpower underresourcing. Either of those conditions in the absence of the other would require deeper probing to determine whether manpower inputs are a root cause. Normal time on the job combined with strong performance metrics would signal adequate or perhaps even excessive manpower resourcing. If manpower underresourcing is indicated, additional analysis is needed to further isolate the root cause. The most likely possibilities are a flawed manpower standard, conscious risk taken in the programming process, or risk taken in MAJCOMs' distribution of funded authorizations.

Figure 7.1. COLS Performance Metrics for the Financial Management Function

Sub Mission Area: Travel Pay (Manual)

Description: Provides full-spectrum manual travel voucher support through the Air Force Financial Services Center, PCS and non-DTS travel vouchers

Reference	Standard	Lvl	Performance		Calculation
			Target	Minimum	
	Variable Standard:				
FM 1.1 Weight: 20	Percent of travel claim payments made to Airmen within 30 days of receipt of travel claim	1	100%	95%	(# of valid travel claim payments made to Airmen within 30 days of receipt of valid travel claim ÷ Total # of valid travel claim payments made to Airmen) * 100 = %
		2	95%	90%	
		3	90%	85%	
		4	85%	85%	
FM 1.2 Weight: 20	Percent of travel vouchers rejected after submission by FSO	1	0%	5%	(# of travel vouchers rejected after submission by FSO ÷ Total # of travel vouchers) * 100 = %
		2	5%	10%	
		3	10%	15%	
		4	15%	20%	

Sub Mission Area: Military Pay

Description: Executes military pay record updates and tracks through Case Management System (CMS)

Reference	Standard	Lvl	Performance		Calculation
			Target	Minimum	
	Variable Standard:				
FM 2.1 Weight: 20	Percent of military pay transactions input within 30 days of effective date of supporting documentation	1	97%	94%	(# of military pay transactions input within 30 days of effective date of supporting documentation ÷ Total # of military pay transactions input) * 100 = %
		2	93%	86%	
		3	85%	76%	
		4	75%	75%	
FM 2.2 Weight: 20	Percent of military pay transactions input correctly	1	97%	94%	(# of military pay transactions input correctly ÷ Total # of military pay transactions input) * 100 = %
		2	93%	86%	
		3	85%	76%	
		4	75%	75%	

Sub Mission Area: Accounting Detail Accuracy

Description: Provides Tri-Annual Review of Commitments, Obligations, Accounts Payable and Accounts Receivable

Reference	Standard	Lvl	Performance		Calculation
			Target	Minimum	
	Variable Standard:				
FM 3.1 Weight: 20	Percent of dormant commitments, unliquidated obligation, accounts payable and accounts receivable transactions reviewed for timeliness, accuracy, and completeness during each of the four month periods ending Jan 31, May 31, and Sep 30	1	97%	96%	(# of dormant commitments, unliquidated obligation, accounts payable and accounts receivable transactions reviewed for timeliness, accuracy, and completeness during the last four-month review period ÷ Total # of dormant commitments, unliquidated obligation, accounts payable and accounts receivable transactions) * 100 = %
		2	95%	91%	
		3	90%	85%	
		4	84%	83%	

SOURCE: Material from AFIMSC/IZ.
NOTES: PCS = permanent change of station; DTS = Defense Travel System; FSO = financial services office.

8. The Management Engineering Workforce

As mentioned in Chapter 4, in addition to the headquarters component located at Joint Base San Antonio–Randolph Air Force Base, Texas, AFMAA has three MRSs located at Joint Base San Antonio–Randolph; Joint Base Langley-Eustis, Virginia; and Peterson Air Force Base, Colorado.[1] The workforce includes a mixture of military and civilians, with the military consisting of mid- to high-grade enlisted and junior officers (with the exception of the MRS commander, usually an O-5). Figure 8.1 shows the numbers and grades of the funded military authorizations and the number and grade of civilians who are assigned to the headquarters AFMAA office and the three MRSs. For example, Headquarters AFMAA has 11 officer positions (lieutenant through colonel), 33 enlisted positions (staff sergeant through chief master sergeant), and 93 civilian positions (GS-7 to GS-15). Most of the civilians AFMAA employs are between the grades of GS-11 and GS-13, with the bulk of the workforce being GS-12s at all locations, with the exception of the 4th MRS at Peterson Air Force Base.

Figure 8.1. AFMAA Military Authorizations and Civilian Inventory

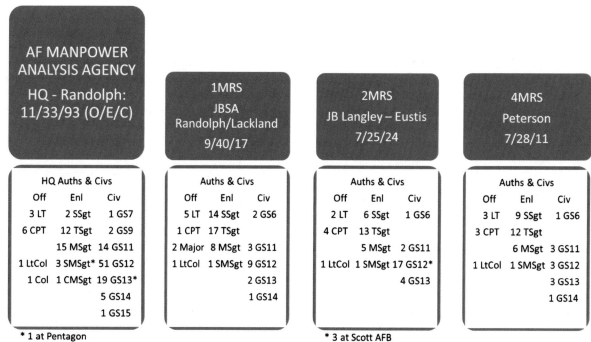

NOTE: Civilian numbers are for those assigned as of August 2018; officer and enlisted numbers are for those authorized as of June 2018.

---

[1] In 2004, when MAJCOM field engineering teams were realigned to AFMAA they were organized into five original squadrons. See the "History" section at Air Force Manpower Analysis Agency, undated.

The funded military authorizations in Figure 8.1 show the military requirements to accomplish the AFMAA mission. It is typical to use civilian personnel assigned instead of civilian authorizations as a measure of the required workforce because of the unreliability of the civilian authorizations in the manpower files. A unit's civilian workforce is not governed strictly by its civilian authorizations, i.e., civilians are not hired solely based on vacant positions. Hiring is constrained by the unit's budget. Although budgets should be linked to civilian authorizations, the execution of that budget determines the workforce more than the authorizations. For military, the funded authorizations are managed as described in Chapters 1 and 2, and the military assignment officers at AFPC decide which positions are manned based on available personnel. Figure 8.2 gives the military manning at Headquarters AFMAA and the MRSs (authorized versus assigned). As of August 2018, only five of the 11 officer positions and 24 of the 33 enlisted positions at Headquarters AFMAA were filled. The MRS positions are filled at a little better rate but are still undermanned in both officers and enlisted. Manning shortages, such as those we observed, put extra pressure on the civilians who typically provide continuity in an organization.

Figure 8.2. AFMAA and MRS Military Manning and Civilian Inventory

Grade	HQ - AFMAA Auth	HQ - AFMAA Asgn	1MRS- Randolph Auth	1MRS- Randolph Asgn	2MRS- Langley Auth	2MRS- Langley Asgn	4MRS- Peterson Auth	4MRS- Peterson Asgn
LT	3	0	5	3	2	1	3	2
Capt	6	3	1	2	4	3	3	1
Major			2	1				
LtCol	1	1	1	1	1	2	1	1
Col	1	1						
Total Off	11	5	9	7	7	6	7	4
SrA				1		1		1
SSgt	2	0	14	10	6	8	9	6
TSgt	12	8	17	15	13	8	12	9
MSgt	15	12	8	8	5	5	6	5
SMSgt	3	3	1	1	1	2	1	1
CMSgt	1	1						
Total Enl	33	24	40	35	25	24	28	22
GS6				2		1		1
GS7		1						
GS9		2						
GS11		14		3		2		3
GS12		51		9		17		3
GS13		19		2		4		3
GS14		5		1				1
GS15		1						
Total Civ		93		17		24		11

NOTE: Civilian numbers are assigned as of August 2018; officer and enlisted numbers are authorized as of June 2018.

The effects of the vacancies in the military manning are somewhat attenuated by the fact that they are predominantly at lower grades (staff sergeant, technical sergeant, lieutenant, and captain). Comparable gaps among more-experienced segments of the workforce would likely be more harmful.

Professionalizing the Management Engineering Workforce

In addition to the numbers of personnel by grade, the types of personnel included in the workforce are important. Since the inception of AFMAA in 1975 as the Air Force Management Engineering Agency, the organization has been responsible for providing technical guidance. It would therefore be expected to have sufficient technical expertise in the workforce. Tables 8.1 and 8.2 show the career fields of the military personnel assigned to AFMAA, combined at the headquarters and at the MRSs. Officers are split evenly between force support (38FX, the former personnel career field), and operation research analyst (61AX), with the squadron commander positions in each MRS being filled by an operations research analyst. Having 11 of the 22 officers from the operations research analyst career field illustrates a dedication to technical expertise. Nearly the entire enlisted workforce is from the manpower (3F3XX) career field (bold). The lower rows in Table 8.2 show the entire enlisted manpower career field to highlight the fact that AFMAA has 97 of the 426 personnel in the career field.

Table 8.1. Military Inventory, AFMAA and MRSs—Officers, by Grade

Air Force Specialty Code	Grade						
	O-1	O-2	O-3	O-4	O-5	O-6	Total
38F1	1	0	0	0	0	0	1
38F3	1	1	3	0	0	0	5
38F4	0	0	2	0	1	0	3
61A1	0	2	1	0	0	0	3
61A3	1	0	2	0	0	0	3
63A3	0	0	0	1	0	0	1
91C0	0	0	0	0	0	1	1
97E0	0	0	1	0	0	0	1
C61A3	0	0	0	0	4	0	4
Total	3	3	9	1	5	1	22

Table 8.2. Military Inventory—Enlisted, by Grade

	Air Force Specialty Code	Grade						
		E-4	E-5	E-6	E-7	E-8	E-9	Total
AFMA and MRSs	2A6X1	0	0	0	1	0	0	1
	2A6X5	0	0	1	0	0	0	1
	2A6X6	0	1	0	0	0	0	1
	3F2X1	0	0	1	0	0	0	1
	3F3X0	**0**	**0**	**0**	**0**	**0**	**1**	**1**
	3F3X1	**3**	**22**	**36**	**28**	**7**	**0**	**96**
	3F5X1	0	1	2	1	0	0	4
	Total	3	24	40	30	7	1	105
Entire enlisted career field	3F3X0	0	0	0	0	0	5	5
	3F3X1	23	109	111	138	40	0	421
	Total	23	109	111	138	40	5	426

Table 8.3 shows that the bulk of the civilian workforce is assigned to the GS-0343 occupation series (management analyst) in the grades of GS-11 to GS-13 (bold row in the table). When combined with Figures 8.1 and 8.2, it illustrates limited ability for promotion at Headquarters AFMAA and at the three MRSs (where nearly all billets are at the GS-12 level).

AFMAA's civilian workforce brings little in terms of technical modeling skills. Table 8.3 shows that no GS-1515 (operations research) personnel are employed anywhere in AFMAA. One GS-0896 (industrial engineer) is employed at AFMAA, and that GS-12 works at one of the MRS locations, perhaps with limited opportunity to share skills and abilities with the others in AFMAA.

Combining the 11 operations research analyst officer positions (three of which are O-5 commanders and, presumably, have leadership and administrative duties to fill most of their time) with the one civilian industrial engineer yields 12 technical analysts out of a total workforce of 273 personnel, roughly 4 percent.

A large portion of the AFMAA workforce is enlisted personnel, most of whom have not completed bachelor's or master's degrees (see Figure 8.3). The Headquarters AFMAA enlisted workforce has slightly more academic education than those assigned to the three squadrons.

At first blush, enlisted members with master's degrees and even bachelor's degrees might seem like a technical workforce when enlisted members are only required to have associate's degrees for promotion purposes. However, the academic specialties of the enlisted personnel at the MRS and Headquarters AFMAA are nearly all in nontechnical fields (see Appendix C). The exceptions might be the training enlisted members get as part of their career field or the associate's degree in manpower, personnel, and training analysis. This level of training and

Table 8.3. AFMAA Civilian Inventory

Occupational Series		Grade								
		GS-6	GS-7	GS-09	GS-11	GS-12	GS-13	GS-14	GS-15	Total
GS-0203	Human resources assistant	0	1	0	0	0	0	0	0	1
GS-0301	Miscellaneous administration and program series	0	0	1	0	0	0	0	0	1
GS-0303	Miscellaneous clerk and assistant	3	0	0	0	0	0	0	0	3
GS-0318	Secretary	1	0	0	0	0	0	0	0	1
GS-0343	**Management analyst**	**0**	**0**	**1**	**16**	**69**	**27**	**6**	**1**	**120**
GS-0501	Financial administration and program	0	0	0	0	0	1	0	0	1
GS-0560	Budget analyst	0	0	0	0	1	0	0	0	1
GS-0896	Industrial engineer	0	0	0	0	1	0	0	0	1
GS-1750	Instructional systems	0	0	0	0	2	0	0	0	2
GS-1801	General inspection, investigation, enforcement, and compliance	0	0	0	0	1	0	1	0	2
GS-2210	Information technology management	0	0	0	6	6	1	0	0	13
	Total	4	1	2	22	80	29	7	1	146

Figure 8.3. AFMAA Enlisted Academic Education Level

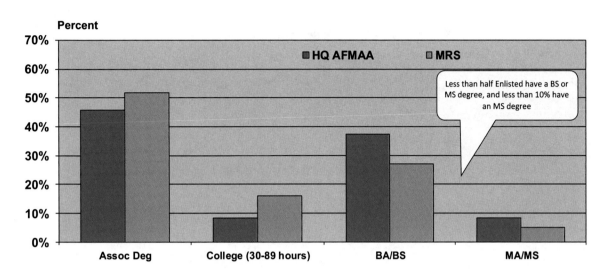

education undoubtedly provides basic analysis skills, which are not likely to include the type of modeling that a more rigorous degree in operations research or industrial engineering would provide. However, as within many engineering-related fields of work, technicians have a proper role and perform valuable tasks within the enterprise. A surveyor need not be a certified civil engineer; likewise, a manpower NCO whose role is to collect data need not be an industrial engineer or degreed operations researcher.

Another aspect of the AFMAA military workforce is their relatively brief tenures in the management engineering function. One tour in AFMAA is common, with tour lengths over multiple decades averaging 3.5 years for enlisted personnel and 2.9 years for officers (see Figure 8.4). We heard in our interviews with MRS personnel that enlisted members generally have no management engineering training prior to their assignment to the MRS, require one to two years to reach a fully qualified level, and tend to have too little time remaining in the assignment after reaching that level.

The largest part of the AFMAA workforce consists of civilians, which is arguably the easiest part of the workforce in which to build and maintain technical expertise. Appropriate adjustment of position descriptions and hiring practices could yield a more highly technical civilian workforce. However, as Table 8.4 shows, nearly 80 percent of the current civilian workforce had prior enlisted experience in the Air Force.[1] As Figure 8.5 indicates, education levels among civilians with prior military service are somewhat lower than those without prior military service. Moreover, data in Appendix C indicate that degrees for both prior- and non–prior-service employees tend to be nontechnical. We found one civilian with a bachelor's degree in industrial

---

[1] We were unable to determine whether any of the remaining civilians had prior military experience in another military service.

engineering (no operations research degrees) and one with three years of college in mechanical engineering among all the civilians working at AFMAA.

Figure 8.4. Military Tour Lengths in AFMAA

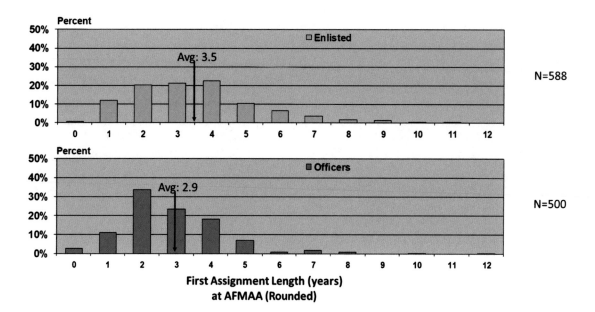

Table 8.4. AFMAA Civilians with Prior Air Force Enlisted Experience

Civilian Grade	Never Enlisted		Highest Achieved Enlisted Grade						Total
	Number	Percent	E-4	E-5	E-6	E-7	E-8	E-9	
GS-06	3	75						1	4
GS-07						1			1
GS-09			1			1			2
GS-11	6	27		1	3	9	2	1	22
GS-12	12	15	1	4	10	33	14	6	80
GS-13	8	28	1	2	2	6	5	5	29
GS-14	1	14				3	2	1	7
GS-15				1					1
Total	30	21	3	8	15	53	23	14	146
Percent			2	5	10	36	16	10	

NOTE: Overall, 40 percent of the Air Force management analyst (GS-0343) occupational series have had prior enlisted experience.

82

Figure 8.5. AFMAA Civilian Academic Education Level

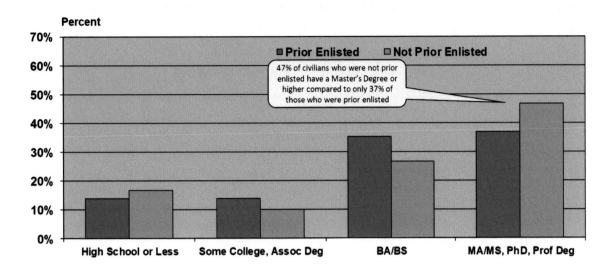

Civilianizing the Management Engineering Workforce

One avenue toward a more-experienced and technically qualified workforce is conversion of most military positions to civilian positions. However, to have the intended results, many existing civilian positions and those converted from military positions would have to be realigned into more-technical occupational series, and hiring practices would have to change to increase emphasis on technical qualifications.

One of the arguments against conversion of military positions to civilian is that military presence and experience is important for AFMAA analysts to understand the organizations they are evaluating. We note, however, that there is low likelihood of a study team member being assigned to a study in a function in which he or she has prior experience. However, enlisted members may have been assigned to manpower flights in force support squadron bases across the Air Force and, therefore, bring an operational perspective.

Additionally, we heard that the military personnel are needed because the workforce must deploy. Tables 8.5 and 8.6 are snapshots of deployment data from June 2018 for military personnel then assigned to AFMAA and the MRSs and compare those numbers with those for all other officers in their career fields during their current assignments. The tables show that only one currently assigned officer had deployed, but if that officer were not available for deployment, the effect on the 38F career field would have been negligible. AFMAA E-6s and E-7s did contribute to meeting deployment demands; if they had not been available, deployment rates would have gone up from 13 percent to 22 percent for E-6s and from 21 percent to 29 percent for E-7s. However, in more-strenuous deployment demand scenarios, such as the first five years after September 11, 2001, shifting AFMAA's expeditionary tasking burden exclusively to force support squadron resources would portray a different picture. We recommend that wartime manpower management concepts of operation be evaluated to determine whether civilian or military reach-back could mitigate effects on a small workforce.

Table 8.5. AFMAA and MRS Enlisted Members Deployed in Current Assignment

	3F3XX Control Air Force Specialty Code—Permanent Party	
Grade	AFMAA	All Other
E-4	0% (0/3)	14% (3/22)
E-5	0% (0/22)	8% (7/91)
E-6	21% (7/34)	13% (9/72)
E-7	29% (8/28)	21% (24/112)
E-8	0% (0/7)	3% (1/32)
E-9	0% (0/1)	0% (0/5)

NOTE: Based on raw AFMAA data as of June 20, 2018.

Table 8.6. AFMAA and MRS Officers Deployed in Current Assignment

	38F Core Identifier—Permanent Party		61A Core Identifier—Permanent Party	
Grade	AFMAA	All Others	AFMAA	All Others
O-1	0% (0/1)	1% (1/129)	0% (0/1)	0% (0/50)
O-2	0% (0/1)	7% (12/166)	0% (0/2)	2% (1/47)
O-3	17% (1/6)	15% (66/439)	0% (0/3)	10% (12/123)
O-4	N/A (0/0)	7% (14/193)	N/A (0/0)	14% (14/97)
O-5	0% (0/1)	6% (13/233)	0% (0/3)	10% (9/87)
O-6	N/A (0/0)	5% (6/116)	N/A (0/0)	6% (1/18)

NOTE: Based on raw AFMAA data as of June 20, 2018.

There are other potential methods for professionalizing the manpower workforce. Shifting a portion of existing military or civilian resources toward more-technical degree credentials could yield improvements. Placing more 61A officers within manpower activities could also provide an infusion of acumen. Another route to improve the professionalism of AFMAA's workforce would involve adjusting the existing training curricula to better address the technical aspects of developing manpower standards. In addition, some career fields have introduced a certification and credentialing structure for their workforces so that skills and experience can be tracked and used in assigning and developing individuals. The manpower career field could implement a similar system for the military and civilian workforces.

9. Conclusions and Recommendations

With a focus primarily on the use of manpower standards or other determinants for ACS manpower requirements, we found Air Force processes to be more comprehensive and technically sophisticated than those most private- or public-sector organizations use for their administrative and support functions. However, we also found that the Air Force processes are less efficient and effective than they could be, and our review suggested a number of steps that the Air Force should take toward improvement.

What Other Organizations Do Better

The best examples we found of effective processes were those for generating force (support) functions of the Army and shore installation functions of the Navy. In both cases, task time and frequency data are collected as a basis for workforce requirements models. However, in both cases, data collection is accomplished primarily through virtual processes (video conferences, data-collection tools) rather than face-to-face SME workshops. This provides a number of advantages:

- larger sample sizes, facilitating greater precision in estimating manpower needs and greater potential replicability of developed standards
- clearer and more consistent instructions to SMEs on how to estimate inputs
- collection from SMEs while they are proximate to the work being performed
- less concern about group dynamics affecting the estimates
- better context for individual estimates
- auditability of inputs through cross-location comparisons
- improved ability to follow up on outliers
- improved identification of needs for variances
- reduced time and labor to execute a manpower study
- reduced travel budget, facilities demands, and scheduling burdens related to workshops
- greater throughput at current resource levels.

The Air Force should further investigate either the Navy process or a hybrid that combines the Navy survey approach with a follow-up workshop of much shorter duration than the current version. A pilot program could be implemented to test these methods, assessing the resources expended and the quality of the result.

Furthermore, we found that both the Army and the Navy hold organizations responsible for developing standards. The Navy has two commands with installation support responsibilities, each with its own manpower function. The Army has many functional commands (with responsibilities somewhat akin to those of Air Force functional managers) with force-generating responsibilities and their own manpower capabilities but also has an agency (USAMAA) that serves a consulting and certification function. The Air Force, by policy, holds functions responsible for manpower standards but, in practice, holds AFMAA and AF/A1M responsible for initiating and managing most studies and producing defensible standards. By holding functional managers responsible for standards, giving AFMAA a consulting and certifying role, and allowing the lack of a certified standard to have negative consequences in programming decisions, the Air Force could significantly reduce the phenomenon of pocket vetoes by functional managers who obstruct or delay the process because they dislike the outcomes of proposed standards. Standards could be reviewed periodically (e.g., every two to three years) to ensure that decisionmakers have current standards with which to accurately adjust the size and structure of the force.

Other organizations in both the public and private sectors tend to collect data and do modeling using workforces that are typically professionally qualified. The educational qualifications of such individuals run more toward management engineering and operations research, and their experience levels tend to be high. While the Air Force AFMAA and MRS civilian workforces tend to be similarly high on experience, we found analytic skills to be thinly available, particularly among the NCOs and former NCOs reemployed as civilians, and we found the NCO components to be very low on experience because of their relatively brief tenures in MRSs. The Air Force's reliance on what is largely a paraprofessional management engineering workforce rather than on a more technically qualified workforce appears to limit the manpower community's ability to focus more on data analysis and model formulation.

Several arguments surfaced to support the need for an NCO contingent in the management engineering workforce. One argument is the need for deployable resources. However, we found deployment demands for manpower specialists at the moment to be low, and reachback for much of what they would do in forward locations is a possibility to be explored. Another is the need for familiarity with the functions being studied. However, we found that the chances of an NCO being assigned to study a function in which he or she had previous experience are very slim, even while a fresh infusion of field operational perspective and knowledge might, in some ways, be useful. Additionally, if a more civilianized AFMAA continued to employ large numbers of veterans, a diversity of functional experiences would still be available in the workforce.

We also question the rationale for the present allocation of the workforce among AFMAA and three MRSs. The Air Force should review the distribution of the manpower workforce to optimize mission accomplishment and interaction with functional communities. Consolidation, for example, may yield economies of scale and would increase analytic rigor and consistency. A move toward virtual rather than face-to-face processes would further reduce the need for dispersal. The spectrum of options involving AFMAA's organizational architecture and geographic dispersion is worthy of follow-on examination.

Our Analysis of Current Policies and Methods

We analyzed several technical aspects of Air Force manpower standard development practices. Our findings pertain to both development of standards and their application.

Manpower Standard Development

In addition to endorsing the survey approach the Navy uses, we saw room for improvement in manpower standard modeling. We recommend the following:

- When feasible, regression estimates should be derived from as many applicable locations as possible, not just the sample of locations represented by SMEs at workshops.
- For functions in which a poor linear relationship between workloads and workload factors is found, nonlinear models and machine learning or artificial intelligence approaches should be considered.
- Where practical, regression or other methods should be used in lieu of the ratio method.
- Statistical best practices should be observed for any model used in developing a manpower standard.

If functional managers are effectively held responsible for their standards, somewhat comparable to what we observed in the Army and Navy, several advantages may be realized. Process mapping, development of standard work documents, and continuous process improvement could be realigned as functional managers' responsibilities and could become prerequisites for constructing or updating a standard. Functional managers could choose among several sources for developing standards—AFMAA analysts, consultant contractors, or their own staffs. The motivation for functional managers to maintain a valid, up-to-date standard could be established through a policy that programming processes could use a standard to justify resources only if it is certified by AFMAA. Policy would need to be established to require that standards be reviewed, renewed, or recertified periodically and would be subject to decertification if mission or technological changes significantly altered the workload factors in the standards.

As we observed in other organizations, the management engineering workforce could be professionalized by shifting more NCO positions to civilian positions and classifying a much larger proportion of positions in analytic job series, with their attendant education requirements. To provide greater retention and development of needed experience within the civilian workforce, positions could be career-ladder graded, with entry at grade GS-7 and automatic promotions to GS-9 and GS-11 at specified intervals, contingent on acceptable performance.

Availability Factors and Other Adjustments

We found that MAFs capture most sources of nonavailable time objectively and with timely updates. However, we found that some sources are not adequately accounted for. The most commonly voiced concern was deployments from garrison forces. However, as we will discuss later, we did not find that MAFs were the appropriate place to capture nonavailability that is due to deployment. We noted that nonavailability that is due to family days and PTDY (e.g., for house hunting or family leave) are not currently captured but that efforts are being made to identify suitable data sources for them.

We found that the Air Force has applied the overload factor, used originally in conjunction with rounding rules to prevent undue per-position burdens in small units, in a way that effectively creates a 43-hour workweek as the basis for manpower standards. This leaves either less available overtime capacity or a higher level of workforce stress for fluctuations in workload, workforce availability, or shortages that are due to resource constraints. We recommend increasing transparency in recognizing this risk and considering policy and programming changes to mitigate the risk. Immediate reversion of the overload factor to its previous form would increase the number of unfunded authorizations as manpower standards are reapplied. The unfunded authorizations would then compete for resources, as we will discuss later.

Deployment Credit

Since 2014, deployments have effectively reduced garrison manpower by about 5,000 spaces, and this effect was even larger in earlier years. Air Force manpower policies have provisions for deployment credit, but these were not implemented because of the resources required to fund the additional manpower and also because the policies provided only static resources to offset dynamically shifting requirements. We recommend establishing a pool of dynamically shifted authorizations to be placed in units during periods of projected deployment taskings. The pool could be managed by the same officials responsible for assigning deployment taskings (currently AFPC), with normal rotational assignments and separations used to keep strengths in line with fluctuating unit-level requirements. We found enough stability and predictability in deployment taskings to make this approach feasible, particularly for high-density requirements.

Feedback Loops

We found that manpower processes lack objective, systematic feedback loops for determining whether adequate manpower requirements are being established. Available feedback comes largely from the impressions commanders and functional managers form and unsystematically convey. We recommend a survey approach to capturing time on the job for military members and one source of feedback and have identified ongoing occupational measurement surveys as a good vehicle. Another useful feedback loop would be the performance metrics associated with COLS, although some of these require improvement to be useful for this purpose.

Effects on Programming

We found that, under current practices, manpower standards have a minimal effect on the programming of manpower resources. A manpower standard is applied when it is first developed or updated, but this generally changes only unfunded authorizations. MAJCOM manpower managers rarely reapply standards because of the accurate perception that changes will generally occur only in unfunded requirements and that unfunded requirements are not routinely used (as we believe they should be) to assess risk and influence programming or policy decisions. We recommend making unfunded authorizations routinely visible in programming processes and levying clear expectations, as appropriate, on manpower managers, functional managers, or programmers at the Air Staff and MAJCOM levels to take such actions as changing work requirements in the standard work document, explicitly reducing levels of service, adopting a longer workweek, increasing funded authorizations, or directing other resources (civilian employees, contractors, or reservist man-days) to the function. To enable more frequent reapplication of standards, we recommend streamlining the process by embedding models in updatable tools and displaying unfunded requirements at the aggregate or abbreviated level of detail.

Summary

We recognize that addressing the inefficiencies uncovered in the management engineering processes for ACS functions will take time, effort, and resources. However, rather than abandoning these processes, we believe the Air Force's interests would be best served by taking available steps to make the process more effective, efficient, and relevant to programming decisions.

A. Manpower Standard Implementation Codes

Table A.1. Manpower Standard Implementation Codes

MSI Category	MSI Code	MSI Definition	Authorizations
Manpower standard	C	(ANG & Reserve only) Manpower standard and UTC requirement	18,157
	G	Manpower standard	98,473
	H	Air Force–approved legacy manpower standard	38,608
	J	MAJCOM-approved legacy manpower standard	12,390
Crew ratio	F	Crew ratio	15,374
LCOM	L	LCOM capability manpower standard	53,905
Technical estimate	X	Medical product line analysis transition team (Platt)–based technical estimate	34,246
	Y	Technical estimate	7,562
UTC	T	UTC requirement (ANG/Reserve use only)	122,477
Headquarters staffs	D	Above wing headquarters staff and covered by manpower standard	1,458
	E	Above wing headquarters staff and sized by a service level	24,543
	N	Outside Air Force	27,363
IMA	V	IMA (Reserve use only)	8,230
Other	B	Foreign military sales	4,077
	M	Competitive sourcing (MEO determined)	2,040
	K	Not covered by manpower standard but agreed through memorandum of understanding or treaty	12,835
	A	Non-A76 contractor manpower equivalent requirement	158
	Q	Not covered by manpower standard, but workload is Air Force directed	44,871
	R	Not covered by manpower standard, but workload is MAJCOM directed	37,470
	W	Deployment participation—MAJCOM funded	179
	Z	Pending validation	88,645
		Total	653,061

SOURCE: MPES data extract for October 2017.
NOTE: Data are for FY 2017. MEO = most efficient organization.

B. Calculation and Simulation Details

In Chapter 4, we discussed how time and frequency estimates are aggregated at each location to produce the total monthly functional man-hours required and described results from a simulation of how the required man-hours are determined. In this appendix, we provide additional details for each of these discussion points.

Calculation of Required Man-Hours

Within a function, each process $p \in \{1, \ldots, P\}$ consists of n_p individual component tasks $k_{ip} \in \{1, \ldots, n_p\}$. Each task has a true average task time, t_{kip}. Some tasks are not performed with every instance of a process, subject to the determination of a decision rule within the process map. To capture that information, we consider each task t_{kip} to also have a true task proportion w_{kip}, with $w_{kip} = 1$ for tasks that are not subject to a decision rule and $0 < w_{kip} < 1$ for tasks that are decision-rule dependent. The workshop produces estimates for each task average time $\hat{t}_{kip}$ and each task proportion $\hat{w}_{kip}$. The true process time, s_p, may then be estimated by $\hat{s}_p$, the sum of all process estimated task times and proportions:

$$\hat{s}_p = \sum_{i=1}^{n_p} \hat{w}_{kip} \cdot \hat{t}_{kip}.$$

For each workshop location, $h \in \{1, \ldots, L\}$, each process p has a regular (monthly) frequency f_{ph}, which either may be known, via historical record or directed requirement, or may be estimated. Assuming all frequencies are known, the (monthly) man-hours y_h required at location h, y_h, may be estimated by summing over process times and frequencies:

$$\hat{y}_p = \sum_{p=1}^{P} f_{ph} \cdot \hat{s}_p.$$

For any process for which the true frequency is estimated, f_{ph} is replaced by its estimated value, $\hat{f}_{ph}$. These monthly man-hour estimates then become the dependent variable in regression-based estimates of the manpower standard, as discussed in Chapter 4.

Simulation Algorithm

In this section, we discuss how the simulations presented in Chapter 4 were generated. The parameters of the simulation here are cited for the example discussed in Chapter 4. This is just one of an infinite set of options for these parameter values. The simulations inform the relative accuracy of a manpower standard for a hypothetical function generated through the algorithm. They guide a discussion of how the current process may induce error rather than attempting to quantify the actual error experienced in the current process.

Initially, the number of locations and the number of processes are set; in this example, there are 75 locations and 80 processes. For each process, the number of tasks is drawn from a Discrete Uniform(5,20) distribution. The number of workshop SMEs is set to ten.

After the number of locations and processes is set, the algorithm progresses in three stages. First, true values of task time, task weights (for decision point–dependent tasks), and frequency are established. These values represent the target actual manpower need predicted by the standard. Then, optionally, measurement error may be induced for task time, weight, or frequency. Finally, a regression model is fit to establish the standard.

Part 1, Set True Time and Frequency Values for Each Process at Each Location

True average task times for each individual task are drawn from a trimodal mixture distribution representing short, medium, and long task-length categories. First, a task length is drawn from a multinomial distribution with probabilities of 0.25, 0.70, and 0.05 of drawing a short, medium, or long task, respectively. Then, conditional on the task-length category, short tasks are drawn from a Gamma(2,1) distribution, medium tasks from a Normal(8,2^2) distribution, and long tasks from a Normal(30,10^2) distribution. Local deviations to each average task time at each location are drawn from a uniform distribution of plus or minus 10 percent of the true average time. The unit of time is minutes; the true averages may, of course, be real numbers representing fractions of minutes.

The probability that execution of a individual task is decision-rule dependent is set at 0.10, and a Bernoulli(0.10) random draw is made for each task. If the random draw selects a task as decision-rule dependent, the proportion at which it occurs across all instances of the process across all locations is drawn from a Beta(3,25) distribution, which heavily favors proportions closer to zero. Similar to the local task times, local deviations to the proportion of time in which a decision-rule dependent task occurs are drawn from a uniform distribution of plus or minus 10 percent of the overall proportion.

The frequency of each process at each location is set through a three-step process. First, a random weight for each process is drawn; this represents each process as a proportion of all processes performed over all locations. This is created by first making a random uniform draw for each process between bounds that express the spread of the task frequencies; bounds are set at 1 and 5 in the example. These individual draws are scaled by the sum of all the draws to produce the weight. Individualized local weights are drawn for each process that are allowed to deviate uniformly from the overall weight by plus or minus 10 percent. The local weights are then rescaled locally to sum to one. In the second step, a frequency total for each location is drawn from a Discrete Uniform distribution between 300 and 3,000. Then, in the final step, the process weights are applied to the frequency total at each location to provide individual process frequencies at each location. These location process frequencies are rounded to the nearest integer.

Once all times, weights, and frequencies are established, they may be aggregated to record a man-hour need for each location. These are the simulated true values that manpower estimates from the standard are attempting to recover. After these values are recorded, a set of locations of the appropriate number is randomly selected to provide to workshop SMEs. A workshop average of the true task times (and proportions for decision-rule–dependent tasks) may then be calculated. The recorded workshop average is rounded to the nearest minute, which is the typical level of recording, and the workshop decision-point proportions are rounded to the nearest whole percentage.

Part 2, Optional Error in Time and Frequency Estimation

The simulation algorithm allows for an options module that can build measurement error into the workshop time estimates. In the examples discussed in Chapter 4 identified to have measurement errors, an underestimation of the location times in the SME estimates was set at 10 percent for tasks longer than 2 minutes. Similarly, an underestimation in decision-rule–dependent task proportions of 10 percent is also present. Finally, when used, measurement errors in the local process frequencies are also allowed a 10 percent underestimation. In contrast to the local deviations in true time and frequency discussed in the prior section, which are drawn uniformly over a range of up to plus or minus 10 percent, this measurement error, when included, is set at 10 percent for all cases. Once any desired measurement error is infused into the times, weights, and frequencies for each location, these may be aggregated to record an error-based measure of man-hour need for each location.

Part 3, Estimating the Standard Through Regression

To facilitate the regression component, an exogenous single workload factor is created, conditional on the true man-hour need at each location, such that a desired true R^2 is established. The marginal distribution of the workload factor is set as Normal($80,30^2$). The correlation between the workload factor and the man-hours is set to the R^2; 0.85 in the example. The conditional distribution of the workload factor, given the distribution of man-hours (assumed to be Normal), is then used to randomly draw a corresponding workload factor for each location's true man-hours, such that the desired correlation is achieved. Using the SME locations, the regression line establishing the standard is then fit.

The simulation is run once all these inputs have been established. Chapter 4 discusses two versions of this simulation. The first uses a single run, with measurement error, to illustrate how regression-based manpower standards derived from small samples may be biased relative to true relationships when time, frequency, and proportion are reported with error, as SMEs might do in the workshops. The second uses 10,000 replications of the simulation to inform error rates in the predicted manpower need from regression-based manpower standards. In the latter case, the error at a location is found by first calculating the absolute value of the difference between the true required man-hours and that predicted by the regression line, and then dividing that difference by the true required manpower.

C. Management Engineering Workforce Academic Degrees

This appendix provides information on the academic degrees held by members of the Headquarters AFMAA and MRS workforces, as discussed in Chapter 8. In all these tables, the academic specialties are rendered as they are in the source database.

Table C.1. MRS Enlisted Academic Specialties

Academic Specialty	Education Level			
	Associate Degree	30–89 Semester Hours	BA/BS	MA/MS
CRIMINAL JUSTICE			4	1
BUS ADM/MGT OTHER				1
HLTH-CARE-MGT				1
LEADERSHIP				1
ARTS HUMANITIES AND EDUC			2	
BUS ADM/MGT ORG MGT			2	
GENERAL/LIBERAL STUDIES			2	
HUM RES MGT/PERS ADM	5	2	1	
ALLIED HEALTH SCIENCES			1	
BUS ADM/MGT GEN MGT OTHER			1	
BUS ADM/MGT PERSOTHER			1	
COMPUTER COMMUNICATIONS			1	
COMPUTER INFO SYSTEMS			1	
ENGINEERING			1	
F&A ART H-ECOM JOURNALISM			1	
HOSP ADM-ADM-HSP SVS ADMIN			1	
PSYCHOLOGY			1	
TECH-MGT			1	
WORKFORCE EDUCATION & DEVELOPMENT			1	
ACFT MAINT TECHNOLOGY	5	3		
INTELL ANALYSIS	1	2		
POLICE-SCI		2		
MPWR PERS & TNG ANALY	20	1		
CONSTN-TRDS-TECH		1		
EMERGENCY MANAGEMENT		1		
SPACE TECHNOLOGY		1		
AIR TRAFFIC CONTROL	1			
BUS ADM/MGT LOGISTICS MGT	1			
EDUC ADM FUNC ED ADM&MGT	1			
ELEC-PWR-TECH	1			

Academic Specialty	Education Level			
	Associate Degree	30–89 Semester Hours	BA/BS	MA/MS
ELECTRONIC SYS TECHNOLOGY	1			
INFO RESOURCES MGT	1			
INFORMATION SYSTEMS MGT	1			
METL-WRKG-TECH	1			
MUNITIONS SYSTEM TECHNOLOGY	1			
SYS TECH AIRCRAFT ARMAMENT	1			
VEHICLE-MAINT	1			
Total	42	13	22	4

SOURCE: Military Personnel Data System extract, June 30, 2018.

Table C.2. Headquarters AFMAA Enlisted Academic Specialties

Academic Specialty	Education Level			
	Associate Degree	30-89 Semester Hours	BA/BS	MA/MS
BUS ADM AND MANAGEMENT			3	1
POL SCI COMP GOV OTHER				1
AERONAUTICAL TECHNOLOGY			1	
BUS ADM/MGT ORG MGT			1	
BUS ADM/MGT STAT PROBABILIT			1	
BUS ADMIN/COMPUTER/INFO SYS			1	
PSYCH PSYCHOLOGY OTHER			1	
RELIGION			1	
MPWR PERS & TNG ANALY	7	1		
INFO RESOURCES MGT	1	1		
HUM RES MGT/PERS ADM	2			
GENERAL/LIBERAL STUDIES	1			
Total	11	2	9	2

SOURCE: Military Personnel Data System extract, June 30, 2018.

Table C.3. MRS Civilian Academic Specialties

Academic Specialty	Education Level			
	High School or Less	Some College, Assoc. Deg	BA/BS	MA/MS, Ph.D., Prof. Deg
Not Prior Enlisted Civilians				
BUSINESS ADMINISTRATION MANAGEMENT&OPERATIONS OTHER (520299)			1	2
PUBLIC ADMINISTRATION (440401)				2
HUMAN RESOURCES MANAGEMENT/PERSONNEL ADMIN GEN(521001)				1
INFORMATION SCIENCE/STUDIES (110401)				1
STRATEGIC INTELLIGENCE (290202)				1
INDUSTRIAL ENGINEERING (143501)			1	
UNKNOWN	2	2		
Total	2	2	2	7
Prior Enlisted Civilians				
BUSINESS ADMINISTRATION AND MANAGEMENT GENERAL (520201)			1	3
HUMAN RESOURCES MANAGEMENT AND SERVICES OTHER (521099)				2
COMPUTER AND INFORMATION SCIENCES GENERAL (110101)			2	1
BUSINESS ADMINISTRATION MANAGEMENT&OPERATIONS OTHER (520299)			1	1
AERONAUTICS/AVIATION/AEROSPACE SCI&TECH GENERAL (490101)				1
BUSINESS MANAGEMENT MARKETING&RELATED SUPPRT SVCS OTH(529999)				1
HUMAN RESOURCES DEVELOPMENT (521005)				1
PROJECT MANAGEMENT (520211)				1
BUSINESS/COMMERCE GENERAL (520101)			2	
AERONAUTICAL/AEROSPACE ENGINEERING TECH/TECHNICIAN (150801)			1	
COMPUTER&INFO SYSTEMS SECURITY/INFORMATION ASSURANCE (111003)			1	
EDUCATION GENERAL (130101)			1	
INDUSTRIAL TECHNOLOGY/TECHNICIAN (150612)			1	
INFORMATION TECHNOLOGY (110103)			1	
PSYCHOLOGY GENERAL (420101)			1	
WEB PAGE DIGITAL/MULTIMEDIA&INFO RESOURCES DESIGN (110801)			1	
AIRFRAME MECHANICS&AIRCRAFT MAINTENANCE TECH/TECHNCN(470607)		1		
BUSINESS OPERATIONS SUPPORT&SECRETARIAL SERVICES OTH (520499)		1		

97

Academic Specialty	Education Level			
	High School or Less	Some College, Assoc. Deg	BA/BS	MA/MS, Ph.D., Prof. Deg
HUMAN RESOURCES MANAGEMENT/PERSONNEL ADMIN GEN(521001)		1		
LIBERAL ARTS AND SCIENCES/LIBERAL STUDIES (240101)		1		
LOGISTICS MATERIALS AND SUPPLY CHAIN MANAGEMENT (520203)		1		
MANAGEMENT INFORMATION SYSTEMS GENERAL (521201)		1		
MISSILE AND SPACE SYSTEMS TECHNOLOGY (290407)		1		
UNKNOWN	6	2		
Total	6	9	13	11

SOURCE: Defense Civilian Personnel Data System extract, August 31, 2018.

Table C.4. Headquarters AFMAA Civilian Academic Specialties

Academic Specialty	High School or Less	Some College, Assoc. Deg	BA/BS	MA/MS, Ph.D., Prof. Deg
Not Prior Enlisted Civilians				
BUSINESS ADMINISTRATION MANAGEMENT&OPERATIONS OTHER (520299)				2
AEROSPACE AERONAUTICAL&ASTRONAUTICAL/SPACE ENGNRNG (140201)				1
HUMAN RESOURCES DEVELOPMENT (521005)				1
HUMAN RESOURCES MANAGEMENT AND SERVICES OTHER (521099)				1
LITERATURE OTHER (231499)				1
PSYCHOLOGY OTHER (429999)				1
BUSINESS ADMINISTRATION AND MANAGEMENT GENERAL (520201)			3	
EDUCATION GENERAL (130101)			1	
HEALTH/HEALTH CARE ADMINISTRATION/MANAGEMENT (510701)			1	
MANAGEMENT SCIENCE (521301)			1	
COMPUTER SYSTEMS NETWORKING AND TELECOMMUNICATIONS (110901)		1		
UNKNOWN	3			
Total	3	1	6	7
Prior Enlisted Civilians				
BUSINESS ADMINISTRATION AND MANAGEMENT GENERAL (520201)			6	7
PUBLIC ADMINISTRATION (440401)				3
INFORMATION TECHNOLOGY (110103)		1	3	2
HUMAN RESOURCES MANAGEMENT AND SERVICES OTHER (521099)			3	2
MANAGEMENT SCIENCE (521301)			1	2
BUSINESS ADMINISTRATION MANAGEMENT&OPERATIONS OTHER (520299)				2
EDUCATIONAL/INSTRUCTIONAL TECHNOLOGY (130501)				2
HUMAN RESOURCES MANAGEMENT/PERSONNEL ADMIN GEN(521001)		3	4	1
EDUCATION OTHER (139999)			1	1
MANAGEMENT INFORMATION SYSTEMS GENERAL (521201)		1		1
ADULT AND CONTINUING EDUCATION ADMINISTRATION (130403)				1
AERONAUTICAL/AEROSPACE ENGINEERING TECH/TECHNICIAN (150801)				1
COMPUTER TECHNOLOGY/COMPUTER SYSTEMS TECHNOLOGY (151202)				1

Academic Specialty	Education Level			
	High School or Less	Some College, Assoc. Deg	BA/BS	MA/MS, Ph.D., Prof. Deg
HUMAN RESOURCES DEVELOPMENT (521005)				1
INTELLIGENCE GENERAL (290201)				1
LOGISTICS MATERIALS AND SUPPLY CHAIN MANAGEMENT (520203)				1
PUBLIC HEALTH GENERAL (512201)				1
SOCIAL SCIENCES GENERAL (450101)				1
AGRONOMY AND CROP SCIENCE (011102)			1	
BUSINESS MANAGEMENT MARKETING&RELATED SUPPRT SVCS OTH(529999)			1	
COMPUTER PROGRAMMING/PROGRAMMER GENERAL (110201)			1	
COMPUTER SYSTEMS NETWORKING AND TELECOMMUNICATIONS (110901)			1	
EARLY CHILDHOOD EDUCATION AND TEACHING (131210)			1	
EDUCATION GENERAL (130101)			1	
FINANCE (520801)			1	
NON-PROFIT/PUBLIC/ORGANIZATIONAL MANAGEMENT (520206)			1	
SOCIOLOGY (161101)			1	
SPORTS AND EXERCISE (360108)			1	
MECHANICAL ENGINEERING (141901)		1		
UNKNOWN	10	1		
Total	10	7	28	31

SOURCE: Defense Civilian Personnel Data System extract, August 31, 2018.

Bibliography

AFI—*See* Air Force Instruction.

AFIMSC—*See* Air Force Installation and Mission Support Center.

AFMAA—*See* Air Force Manpower Analysis Agency.

AFMAN—*See* Air Force Manual.

AFPC—*See* Air Force Personnel Center.

Abe, Tolu K., Benita M. Beamon, Richard L. Storch, and Justin Agus, "Operations Research Applications in Hospital Operations: Part I," *IIE Transactions on Healthcare Systems Engineering*, Vol. 6, No. 1, January 2016a, pp. 42–54.

Abe, Tolu K., Benita M. Beamon, Richard L. Storch, and Justin Agus, "Operations Research Applications in Hospital Operations: Part II," *IIE Transactions on Healthcare Systems Engineering*, Vol. 6, No. 2, March 2016b, pp. 96–109.

———, "Operations Research Applications in Hospital Operations: Part III," *IIE Transactions on Healthcare Systems Engineering*, Vol. 6, No. 3, June 2016c, pp. 175–191.

AFMAA—*See* Air Force Manpower Analysis Agency.

AFIMSC—*See* Air Force Installation and Mission Support Center.

Agency for Healthcare Research and Quality, "Patient Safety Primer: Nursing and Patient Safety," webpage, U.S. Department of Health and Human Services, August 2018. As of September 24, 2018:
https://psnet.ahrq.gov/primers/primer/22/Nursing-and-Patient-Safety

Air Force Doctrine, Annex 4-0, *Combat Support*, Washington, D.C.: U.S. Department of the Air Force, 2015. As of August 22, 2018:
https://www.doctrine.af.mil/Portals/61/documents/Annex_4-0/
4-0-Annex-COMBAT-SUPPORT.pdf

Air Force Guidance Memorandum 2018-90-01, *Air Force Strategy, Planning, Programming, Budgeting and Execution (SPPBE) Process*, Washington, D.C.: U.S. Department of the Air Force, May 31, 2018. As of Apr 29, 2019:
https://www.afacpo.com/AQDocs/afgm2018-90-01.pdf

Air Force Installation and Mission Support Center, "FY19 AF COLS Update," briefing, August 18, 2018.

Air Force Instruction 10-401, *Air Force Operations Planning and Execution*, Washington, D.C.: U.S. Department of the Air Force, December 7, 2006, incorporating Change 4, March 13, 2012. As of December 8, 2017:
http://static.e-publishing.af.mil/production/1/af_a3_5/publication/afi10-401/afi10-401.pdf

Air Force Instruction 38-101, *Manpower and Organization*, Washington, D.C.: U.S. Department of the Air Force, August 29, 2019. As of March 31, 2020:
https://static.e-publishing.af.mil/production/1/af_a1/publication/afi38-101/afi38-101.pdf

Air Force Instruction 38-201, *Management of Manpower Requirements and Authorizations*, Washington, D.C.: U.S. Department of the Air Force, January 30, 2014.

Air Force Instruction 38-401, *Continuous Process Improvement (CPI)*, Washington, D.C.: U.S. Department of the Air Force, April 15, 2016. As of September 12, 2018:
http://static.e-publishing.af.mil/production/1/saf_mg/publication/afi38-401/afi38-401.pdf

Air Force Manual 38-102, *Manpower and Organization Standard Work Processes and Procedures*, Washington, D.C.: U.S. Department of the Air Force, September 4, 2019. As of April 12, 2020:
https://static.e-publishing.af.mil/production/1/af_a1/publication/afman38-102/afman38-102.pdf

Air Force Manual 38-208 Vol. I, *Air Force Management Engineering Program (MEP)—Processes*, Washington, D.C.: U.S. Department of the Air Force, March 29, 2002, incorporating Change 1, December 10, 2007.

Air Force Manual 38-208 Vol. II, *Air Force Management Engineering Program (MEP)—Quantification Tools*, Washington, D.C.: U.S. Department of the Air Force, November 19, 2003.

Air Force Manpower Analysis Agency, fact sheet, undated. As of April 1, 2020:
https://www.af.mil/About-Us/Fact-Sheets/Display/Article/104598/air-force-manpower-agency/

———, *Military Peacetime Man-Hour Availability Factor (MAF) 2016 Report*, Randolph Air Force Base, Tex., March 2017.

Air Force Personnel Center, *Firefighter Man-Hour Availability Factor (MAF) Study Report*, Randolph Air Force Base, Tex., August 2013a.

———, *Civilian Peacetime Man-Hour Availability Factor (MAF) Study Report*, Randolph Air Force Base, Tex., November 2013b.

———, *Final Report for Indirect Allowance Factor*, Randolph Air Force Base, Tex., April 2015.

Army Regulation 570-4, *Manpower Management,* Washington, D.C.: Headquarters Department of the Army, February 8, 2006. As of March 31, 2020:
http://dopma-ropma.rand.org/pdf/AR-570-4.pdf

Army Regulation 71-32, *Force Development and Documentation Consolidated Policies,* Washington, D.C.: Headquarters, Department of the Army, March 20, 2019. As of March 31, 2020:
https://armypubs.army.mil/epubs/DR_pubs/DR_a/pdf/web/ARN8238_AR71_32_FINAL.pdf

Avalere Health LLC, *Optimal Nurse Staffing to Improve Quality of Care and Patient Outcomes: Executive Summary,* Washington, D.C., September 2015. As of April 6, 2020:
https://cdn.ymaws.com/www.anamass.org/resource/resmgr/docs/
NurseStaffingWhitePaper.pdf

Berry, William D., "The Confusing Case of Budgetary Incrementalism: Too Many Meanings for a Single Concept," *Journal of Politics*, Vol. 52, No. 1, February 1990, pp. 167–196.

Broyles, James R., Jeffery K. Cochran, and Douglas C. Montgomery, "A Markov Decision Process to Dynamically Match Hospital Inpatient Staffing to Demand," *IIE Transactions on Healthcare Systems Engineering*, Vol. 1, No. 2, 2011, pp. 116–130.

Code of Federal Regulations, Title 42, Public Health, Ch. IV, Centers for Medicare and Medicaid Services, Department of Health and Human Services, Subch. G, Standards and Certification, Pt. 482, Conditions of Participation for Hospitals, Subpt. A, General Provisions, Sec. 482.23, Condition of Participation: Nursing Services, as amended to September 30, 2019. As of April 6, 2020:
https://www.law.cornell.edu/cfr/text/42/482.23

Coffman, Michael, Lonnie Gregg, and Op Rahul, "Transportation Security Agency Resource Allocation Process Overview," presentation to RAND, TSA Office of Security Operations, Security Operations Coordination Division, January 18, 2018.

Cotten, Ann, *Seven Steps of Effective Workforce Planning*, Washington, D.C.: IBM Center for the Business of Government, 2007.

County of Fairfax, Virginia, *Strategic Workforce Planning*, Fairfax, Va., August 2003.

———, *Comprehensive Annual Financial Report for the Fiscal Year Ending June 30, 2017,* Fairfax, Va.: Department of Finance, June 30, 2017. As of March 31, 2020:
https://www.fairfaxcounty.gov/finance/sites/finance/files/assets/documents/pdf/cafr1/fy2017
cafr.pdf

Damelio, Robert, *The Basics of Process Mapping*, 2nd ed., New York: CRC Press, 2011.

Defense Manpower Data Center, "DoD Personnel, Workforce Reports & Publications," webpage, undated. As of April 8, 2020:
https://www.dmdc.osd.mil/appj/dwp/dwp_reports.jsp

Department of Defense Directive 5010.42, *DoD-Wide Continuous Process Improvement (CPI)/Lean Six Sigma (LSS) Program*, Washington, D.C.: U.S. Department of Defense, May 15, 2008.

Department of the Navy, Department of the Navy Issuances website, undated. As of May 5, 2020:
https://www.secnav.navy.mil/doni/default.aspx

Dreesch, Norbert, Carmen Dolea, Mario R. Dal Poz, Alexandre Goubarev, Orvill Adams, Maru Aregawi, Karin Bergstrom, Helga Fogstad, Della Sheratt, Jennifer Linkins, Robert Scherpbier, and Mayada Youssef-Fox, "An Approach to Estimating Human Resource Requirements to Achieve the Millennium Development Goals," *Health Policy and Planning*, Vol. 20, No. 5, September 2005, pp. 267–276.

Edison International, "About Edison International," webpage, undated. As of April 1, 2020:
https://www.edison.com/home/about-us.html

eFinanceManagement, *Incremental Budgeting—Meaning, Advantages, and Disadvantages*, September 22, 2018. As of August 28, 2018:
https://efinancemanagement.com/budgeting/incremental-budgeting

Espinosa-Fernández, Lourdes, Elena Miró, MóCarmen Cano, and Gualberto Buela-Casal, "Age-Related Changes and Gender Differences in Time Estimation," *Acta Psychologica*, Vol. 112, No. 3, March 2003, pp. 221–223.

FBI—*See* Federal Bureau of Investigation.

Federal Bureau of Investigation, *Today's FBI: Facts & Figures 2013–2014*, Washington, D.C.: U.S. Department of Justice, 2014. As of March 31, 2020:
https://www.fbi.gov/file-repository/facts-and-figures-031413-2.pdf/view

Fine, Philip, and Tina Vajsbaher, "How Good Are Groups at Estimating Time?" in Aaron Williamon and Werner Goebl, eds., *Proceedings of the International Symposium on Performance Science 2013*, Brussels: Association Européenne des Conservatoires, 2013, pp. 741–746.

Government Accountability Office, *Aviation Security: TSA Uses Current Assumptions and Airport-Specific Data for its Staffing Process and Monitors Passenger Wait Times Using Daily Operations Data*, Washington, D.C.:, GAO-18-236, February 2018.

Hoffman, Bruce, Edwin Meese III, and Timothy J. Roemer, *The FBI: Protecting the Homeland in the 21st Century*, Washington, D.C.: 9/11 Review Commission, March 2015. As of August

27, 2018:
https://www.jewishvirtuallibrary.org/jsource/Terrorism/911reviewcommission.pdf

Jacobs, Jerry A., "Measuring Time at Work: Are Self-Reports Accurate," *Monthly Labor Review*, Vol. 121, No. 12, December 1998, pp. 42–53.

Kahneman, Daniel, and Amos Tversky, *Intuitive Prediction: Biases and Corrective Procedures*, Arlington, Va.: Cybernetics Technology Office, Defense Advanced Research Projects Agency, 1977. As of March 31, 2020
https://apps.dtic.mil/dtic/tr/fulltext/u2/a047747.pdf

Kruger, Justin, and Matt Evans, "If You Don't Want to Be Late, Enumerate: Unpacking Reduces the Planning Fallacy," *Journal of Experimental Social Psychology*, Vol. 40, No. 5, September 2004, pp. 586–598.

Lehto, Mark, and Steven J. Landry, *Introduction to Human Factors and Ergonomics for Engineers*, 2nd ed., Boca Raton, Fla.: CRC Press, 2012.

Lindblom, Charles E., "The Science of 'Muddling Through,'" *Public Administration Review*, Vol. 19, No. 2, Spring 1959, pp. 79–88.

Lindblom, Charles E., "Still Muddling, Not Yet Through," *Public Administration Review*, Vol. 39, No. 6, 1979, pp. 517–526.

Manning, Michael, "Designing and Launching a Successful Enterprise-Wide Workforce Planning Program," presentation, Rosemead, Calif.: Edison International, November 2012.

Moløkken-Østvold, Kjetil, and Magne Jørgensen, "Group Processes in Software Effort Estimation," *Empirical Software Engineering*, Vol. 9, December 2004, pp. 315–334.

Myny, Dries, Dirk Van Goubergen, Veronique Limère, Micheline Gobert, Sofie Verhaeghe, and Tom Defloor, "Determination of Standard Times of Nursing Activities Based on a Nursing Minimum Dataset," *Journal of Advanced Nursing*, Vol. 66, No. 1, January 2010, pp. 92–102.

Nataraj, Shanthi, Christopher Guo, Philip Hall-Partyka, Susan M. Gates, and Douglas Yeung, *Options for Department of Defense Total Workforce Supply and Demand Analysis: Potential Approaches and Available Data Sources*, Santa Monica, Calif.: RAND Corporation: RR-543-OSD, 2014. As of September 18, 2018:
https://www.rand.org/pubs/research_reports/RR543.html

Navy Manpower Analysis Center, *Navy Total Force Manpower Requirements Handbook*, Millington, Tenn., April 2000. As of May 6, 2020:
https://www.public.navy.mil/bupers-npc/organization/navmac/Documents/ReqHdBk.pdf

Office of the Chief of Naval Operations Instruction 1000.16L, *Navy Total Force Manpower Policies and Procedures*, Change 1, April 28, 2016.

Office of the Chief of Naval Operations Instruction 5440.77B, *Missions, Functions, and Tasks of the United States Fleet Forces Command*, Washington, D.C.: Department of the Navy, April 25, 2012. As of May 7, 2020:
https://www.secnav.navy.mil/doni/Directives/05000%20General%20Management%20Security%20and%20Safety%20Services/05-400%20Organization%20and%20Functional%20Support%20Services/5440.77B.pdf

Office of the Chief of Naval Operations Instruction 5450.339, *Mission, Functions, and Tasks of Commander, Navy Installations Command*, Washington, D.C.: Department of the Navy, April 21, 2011. As of March 31, 2020:
https://www.secnav.navy.mil/doni/Directives/05000%20General%20Management%20Security%20and%20Safety%20Services/05-400%20Organization%20and%20Functional%20Support%20Services/5450.339.pdf

Office of the Inspector General, Department of Justice, *Audit of the Federal Bureau of Investigation Annual Financial Statements Fiscal Year 2017*, December 2017. As of August 23, 2018:
https://oig.justice.gov/reports/2017/a1807.pdf#page=1

Office of Management and Budget Circular A-76, "Performance of Commercial Activities," Washington, D.C.: Executive Office of the President, August 4, 1983, revised 1999.

Oncology Nursing Society, "Legislation Mandating Nurse Staffing Plans and Ratios Remains Controversial," undated.

OPNAVINST—*See* Office of the Chief of Naval Operations Instruction.

Ozcan, Serpil, and Peter Hornby, "Determining Hospital Workforce Requirements: A Case Study," *Human Resources for Health Development Journal*, Vol. 3, No. 3, September–December 1999, pp. 210–220.

Robbert, Albert A., Lisa M. Harrington, Tara L. Terry, and Hugh G. Massey, *Air Force Manpower Requirements and Component Mix: A Focus on Agile Combat Support*, Santa Monica, Calif.: RAND Corporation, RR-617-AF, 2014. As of September 12, 2017:
https://www.rand.org/pubs/research_reports/RR617.html

Rowe, Gene, and George Wright, "The Delphi Technique as a Forecasting Tool: Issues and Analysis," *International Journal of Forecasting*, Vol. 15, No. 4, October 1999, pp. 353–375.

Roy, Michael M., and Nicholas J. S. Christenfeld, "Bias in Memory Predicts Bias in Estimation of Future Task Duration," *Memory and Cognition*, Vol. 35, No. 2, 2007, pp. 557–564.

———, "Effect of Task Length on Remembered and Predicted Duration," *Psychonomic Bulletin & Review,* Vol. 15, No. 1, 2008, pp. 202–207.

Sharma, Kavya, Sanjay P. Zodpey, Abhay Gaidhane, and Syed Zahiruddin Quazi, "Methodological Issues in Estimating and Forecasting Health Manpower Requirement," *Journal of Public Administration and Policy Research*, Vol. 6, No. 2, August 2014, pp. 25–33.

Siddiqui, Sauleh, Elizabeth Morse, and Scott Levin, "Evaluating Nurse Staffing Levels in Perianesthesia Care Units Using Discrete Event Simulation," *IISE Transactions on Healthcare Systems Engineering*, Vol. 7, No. 4, 2017, pp. 215–223.

Sniezek, Janet A., and Rebecca A. Henry, "Revision, Weighting, and Commitment in Consensus Group Judgment," *Organizational Behavior and Human Decision Processes*, Vol. 45, No. 1, February 1990.

Society for Human Resource Management, "Practicing the Discipline of Workforce Planning," webpage, December 21, 2015. As of April 1, 2020: https://www.shrm.org/resourcesandtools/tools-and-samples/toolkits/pages/practicingworkforceplanning.aspx

Thompson, Andrew, "Walmart's HRM: HR Planning, Job Analysis & Design," Panmore Institute website, January 28, 2017. As of August 6, 2018: http://panmore.com/walmart-human-resource-management-planning-job-analysis-design

Tucker, Harvey J., *Incremental Budgeting: Myth or Model?* Western Political Quarterly, Vol. 35, No. 3, 1982, pp. 327–338.

U.S. Army Manpower Analysis Agency, "Introduction to the United States Army Manpower Analysis Agency (USAMAA)," presentation to RAND, U.S. Department of the Army, January 12, 2018.

U.S. Office Personnel Management, *Migration Planning Guidance Information Documents: Workforce Planning Best Practices*, Washington, D.C., October 7, 2011. As of August 1, 2018: https://www.opm.gov/services-for-agencies/hr-line-of-business/migration-planning-guidance/workforce-planning-best-practices.pdf

Weick, Mario, and Ana Guinote, "How Long Will It Take? Power Biases Time Predictions," *Journal of Experimental Social Psychology*, Vol. 46, No. 4, July 2010, pp. 595–604.

World Health Organization, *Workload Indicators of Staffing Need (WISN) User's Manual*, Geneva, Switzerland, 2010. As of April 1, 2020: https://www.who.int/hrh/resources/wisn_user_manual/en/